WEAPONS OF WHITENESS™

EXPOSING THE MASTER'S TOOLS BEHIND THE MASK OF ANTI-BLACKNESS

CATRICE M. JACKSON, MS, LMHP, LPC

INTERNATIONAL BEST-SELLING AUTHOR
AMERICA'S #1 EXPERT ON WHITE WOMAN VIOLENCE

Catriceology
Show Up, Shine & Do The Damn Thing

CATRICE M. JACKSON

Published by Catriceology® Enterprises, LLC
Omaha, NE | United States of America
Copyright © 2020 by Catrice M. Jackson

ALL RIGHTS RESERVED No portion of this publication may be reproduced, stored in any electronic system, or transmitted in any form or by any means, electronic, mechanical, photocopy, recording, or otherwise, without written permission from the author. Brief quotations may be used in literary reviews.

The author has made every effort to ensure the accuracy of the information within this book was correct at the time of publication. The author does not assume and hereby disclaims any liability to any party for any loss, damage, or disruption caused by errors or omissions, whether such errors or omissions result from accident, negligence, or any other cause.

This publication contains the opinions and ideas of its author and other third parties. It is sold with the understanding that neither the author nor the publisher is engaged in rendering medical, health, psychological, or any other kind of personal professional services in the book. If the reader requires personal, medical, health, or other assistance or advice, a competent professional should be consulted.

The author and publisher specifically disclaim all responsibility for any liability, loss, or risk, personal or otherwise, that is incurred as a consequence, directly or indirectly, of the use and application of the contents of this book.

This is a work of non-fiction. However, certain names and details have been omitted or changed, some characters are composites, and dialogue has been edited.

FOR INFORMATION CONTACT:
Catrice M. Jackson, M.S., LMHP, LPC, America's #1 Expert on White Woman Violence, Racial Justice Educator, Speaker, and International Best-Selling Author.

ONLINE ORDERING IS AVAILABLE FOR ALL PRODUCTS:
www.amazon.com

WEBSITES:
www.catriceology.com
www.shetalkswetalk.com
www.catriceologyenterprises.com

ISBN-13: 978-0-9838398-7-3 (Catriceology® Enterprises, LLC)

Book Cover Design: Kerri Liu
Interior Design: Kerri Liu
Editor: Marian Gallagher
Printed in the USA 10 9 8 7 6 5 4 3 2

WEAPONS OF WHITENESS

EXPOSING THE MASTER'S TOOLS BEHIND THE MASK OF ANTI-BLACKNESS

TABLE OF CONTENTS

DEDICATION	IX
FOREWORD	XV
HOW TO USE THIS BOOK	XIX
INTRODUCTION	XXI
CHAPTER 1: WEAPONS OF WHITENESS	2
CHAPTER 2: WEAPONRY 101 | THE WEAPON FORMERLY KNOWN AS FRAGILITY	22
CHAPTER 3: WHITE WOMAN VIOLENCE 101	38
CHAPTER 4: WHITE TERRORISM	60
CHAPTER 5: THE MASTER'S TOOLS	78
CHAPTER 6: BLACK BECKYS AND BRADS	96
CHAPTER 7: BOUNTY HUNTERS	118
CHAPTER 8: BLACK CODES	138
CHAPTER 9: TIME TO GET FREE AND HEAL	156
CHAPTER 10: SEPARATION FOR LIBERATION	172
AFTERWORD	198

RESOURCES

WILLIE LYNCH LETTER	208
WEAPONS OF WHITENESS INVENTORY	222
TYPES OF BECKYS	236
WEAPONS FOR WINNING	240
WE ALL WE GOT | UNF*CKABLEWITH	244
THREE POWERFUL STEPS FOR YOUR HEALING JOURNEY	254
50 WAYS TO BE MORE COURAGEOUS	258
WRITING PROMPTS TO RISE FROM THE ASHES	266
ABOUT THE AUTHOR	300
CONTACT	302

DEDICATION

For Tyson and Tahlia, My Legacy

> I want to live the rest of my life, however long or short,
> with as much sweetness as I can decently manage, loving all the
> people I love, and doing as much as I can of the work I still have
> to do. I am going to write fire until it comes out my ears, my eyes,
> my noseholes—everywhere. Until it's every breath I breathe.
> I'm going to go out like a fucking meteor!
>
> Audre Lorde, *A Burst of Light*

I never really thought about the power of ancestral love and guidance until I became a grandmother. I don't know if I'm thinking about that power more frequently now because I'm moving into the second half of my life, or because I've been intentional about discovering the truth about my ancestral roots. Perhaps it is a beautiful combination of both. Nevertheless, reconnecting to my ancestors' voices and wisdom over the past year has been a profound blessing. It's sobering to realize that one day I too will be an ancestor, and so the question arises, "What kind of ancestor do I want to be?"

When my grandson was born, it was the first time I deeply and intimately thought about my legacy. And I think about it again every time he stands before me and I gaze into his big beautiful eyes. Although I had felt something similar when I gave birth to my only son, somehow looking into Tyson's eyes was different. The gaze hit me differently. For the first time, I imagined my descendants without me. I must admit the thought both warmed my soul and brought tears to my eyes.

Then when my first granddaughter was born in 2020, I felt a special kind of push and pull to spend the rest of my life blazing a trail to create a legacy that my grandchildren would not only be proud of, but also inspired and empowered to follow. I realized I have the opportunity and privilege to create a legacy relationship with her, much like the one I had with my own grandmother (and I sure wish my grandmother were still here to see another generation of her legacy!). I am grateful for the opportunity to be a grandmother like the one I had. I love you, Tyson and Tahlia! I am a voice for racial justice and Black liberation for both of you. And when I become an ancestor, I hope you pick up the baton and run with it, until freedom comes or you create it.

When I think about what my mother, grandmother, and great-grandmother had to endure for justice, freedom, and liberation, it humbles and inspires me to dig deeper into what justice, freedom, and liberation look like for me and my generation. For if it weren't for my ancestors' persistence and resistance, I wouldn't be here today, fighting for my own freedom and liberation and paving a path of freedom for my children and grandchildren. I know my ancestors are jumping for joy and celebrating as they watch me walk out my destiny as a freedom fighter. And it is my joy, pleasure, and duty to be of service to humanity. Thank you, Ancestors, for your blood, sweat, and tears. Your ability to endure unspeakable pain created the path I walk on today, and I am honored to be your wildest dreams. I commit to keeping my boots on the ground and my eyes on freedom until I take my last breath.

The year 2020 is both a sad and exciting time to be alive. Little did we know that one day—specifically, May 25, 2020—a Black man named George Floyd would be the tipping point for the racial justice uprising in America. After a white police officer choked the life out of George Floyd by kneeling on his neck for eight minutes and forty-six seconds, Black America finally said enough is enough! Through protests, rallies, marches, occupations, and demonstrations, the white terroristic power structures are beginning to crack, probably for the first time in American history, and it's a beautiful thing.

My enslaved great-grandmother and grandmother never saw uprisings like this in their lifetimes, but my mother, my only living matriarch, is alive to witness this historic moment and watch her daughter be a part of it. Before George Floyd, there were Trayvon Martin, Michael Brown, Sandra Bland, Tamir Rice, Freddie Gray, Korryn Gaines, Eric Garner, Rekia Boyd, and so many more who were murdered by white terrorism. May they rest in peace knowing their Black lives mattered. I wasn't sure I'd be alive to see any significant change happen for Black people, but here I stand on the shoulders of my ancestors as a participant and witness, and I am grateful.

This book is dedicated to all the Black people who endured chattel slavery, to those who fought for civil rights, and to those who are leading the revolution today. And especially to Black women. We do this work and lead the charge because we love Black people, and I do this work because justice is love. I still have a lot of fire and fight in me, and I will continue to fight the good fight by any means necessary.

Here are just a few of the many Black people who inspire and empower me to keep my boots on the ground. I honor and applaud these Freedom Fighters:

Harriet Tubman	Angela Davis
Nat Turner	Dick Gregory
Ella Baker	Nekima Levy Armstrong
Malcolm X	Chauntyll Allen
Fannie Lou Hamer	Satara Strong
James Baldwin	Raeisha Williams
Audre Lorde	Kimberly Handy-Jones

"We declare our right on this earth to be a human being, to be respected as a human being, to be given the rights of a human being in this society, on this earth, in this day, which we intend to bring into existence by any means necessary."

—Malcolm X

WEAPONS OF WHITENESS

FOREWORD

Nekima Levy Armstrong,
Civil Rights Attorney, Racial Justice Expert, and Activist

In Minneapolis, we are grappling with the aftermath of the murder of George Floyd—another Black man brutally murdered at the hands of the Minneapolis Police, another Black man murdered under the glaring spotlight of the white gaze. Like many major metropolitan areas, Minneapolis suffers from the devastating effects of white supremacy and racism, which permeate every institution, system, neighborhood, and community. Minneapolis consistently ranks as one of the best places for white people to live, while simultaneously ranking as one of the worst places in the country for Black folks to live, across every key indicator of quality of life. Far too many white people are in denial about the fact that their whiteness is literally killing us. We are being choked by the vice grips of poverty, mass incarceration, police violence, racism, inferior education systems, and internalized oppression, which cause us to turn against each other.

For the past several years, Catrice Jackson—anti-racism master trainer, best-selling author, freedom fighter, and visionary—has traveled to Minneapolis and across the country to help usher in a much-needed paradigm shift of racial consciousness. Catrice has been using her unparalleled techniques, knowledge, wisdom, and experience to teach white women about their Weapons of Whiteness, how they routinely wield those weapons, and how they can consciously work to do less harm to Black women, men, and children. Catrice's trainings have literally helped to save lives and change the hearts and minds of white women who were comfortable and complacent with practicing white supremacy (or as Catrice calls it, "white terrorism") and doing harm to Black bodies. Catrice has also invested significant time and energy into helping liberate Black people from the many tentacles of white supremacy through her workshops, books, lectures, and the birthing of Harriet's Dream, a multi-faceted, Black-led institution designed to educate, strengthen, and stretch Black women to reach our fullest potential.

In the spirit of Harriet Tubman, Catrice uses the knowledge and wisdom contained in Weapons of Whiteness to set the captives free and to help us understand the tools white people have been handed to destroy the Black psyche, to stifle Black people's economic and career potential, and in far too many cases, to put Black lives at risk of harm or death. Catrice makes clear that rather than reject these tools of destruction, many Black people have made the dangerous decision to utilize these tools against other Black people, causing immeasurable harm, individually and collectively within the Black community.

Catrice hones in on arguably the four most potent effects of Weapons of Whiteness: to deny, defend, derail, and destroy humanity, specifically Black humanity. These Weapons of Whiteness must be acknowledged, deconstructed, rejected, and detonated by Black people; doing so takes a heightened level of consciousness and intentionality. Black people must be willing to break the cycle of perpetuating anti-blackness and internalized oppression, and resolve to treat other Black people humanely and with dignity. In other words, rather than operate inside the dehumanizing and self-hating box that white supremacy has offered us, resolve to, as Catrice says, "Live free or die trying." Living free requires us to actively challenge and reject white supremacy, while intentionally embracing, promoting, and loving Black history, Black culture, Black power, and Black people. Living free also means actively rejecting stereotypes about Black people, false narratives, and white lies that claim Black pathology is to blame for the dehumanizing conditions we experience in the Black community. Living free means reshaping the narrative to hold white people, white supremacy, and white power responsible for the oppression we experience. Like Harriet Tubman, Catrice urges us to be willing to risk it all to obtain freedom—including our lives, if necessary.

As a civil rights attorney, racial justice expert, and activist on the frontlines fighting for societal change, I wholeheartedly recommend this book to those who are serious about being transformed and set free. It is past time for our people to learn about the key Weapons of Whiteness and the roles they play in keeping us oppressed. Knowledge is power, and as Catrice illustrates throughout this powerful book, we no longer have to remain in bondage to white supremacy. Read this book. Embody it and get free.

HOW TO USE THIS BOOK

My intention for this book, *Weapons of Whiteness*™, is that it be an important tool for you as you start or continue your journey of personal healing, freedom, and liberation. I hope you will read it in its entirety, and then keep it handy as a reference and inspiration.

I recommend that you read each chapter with thoughtful intention. Be open to the ideas I present, but if you disagree with them, be honest with yourself about how you disagree with me and/or what you think is true for you.

As you read, pay attention to what triggers you and why. You may need to dig deep to fully understand how toxic whiteness and anti-blackness are affecting you.

At the end of each chapter, I invite you to lay down your weapons! I have provided the definitions for one or more Weapons of Whiteness, with writing prompts to help you think deeply about these weapons and how they may be appearing in your life. Are they being used against you? Are you using them against others?

The Resources section contains important reference materials. In addition, both the Afterword and the Resources section called "Writing Prompts to Rise From the Ashes" include writing prompts. Use these prompts to help you release and process your feelings around fighting both systemic racism and anti-blackness My hope is that these prompts will allow you to focus more on your healing and joy. I believe it's not only possible, but also necessary and urgent, that each of us rise from the ashes!

INTRODUCTION

THE TRUTH ABOUT WHITENESS

> Ain't nothing supreme about whiteness.
> It is the cesspool of humanity.
>
> Catrice M. Jackson

There is nothing supreme or superior about whiteness. It's not any more special or unique than blackness or brownness, yet some folks believe this delusion. Ever since the Europeans who invaded the continent of North America started calling themselves "white," the fallacy has been that white folks are the superior race. I always laugh when I hear the word "white" used with "supremacy" or "superiority." These hilarious and untrue words do not just form a simple phrase; they create an oxymoron infused with hypocrisy and terror. This is not just my opinion, it is a fact. We can look at history and current events to find proof—although even with a preponderance of evidence, white folks will still act like they don't know what I'm talking about when I say whiteness isn't supreme or superior, it is violent and terroristic.

And when I say "whiteness," I am specifically talking about white folks, folks of European descent. Anyone who is not Black or Brown. When I speak about whiteness, I'm talking about the collective white folks as a group, and yes, I'm generalizing on purpose. Because no other group (aka "race") of people in the United States has been more violent and terroristic than white folks.

No racial group in America has collectively committed as many crimes against humanity as white folks have. Whiteness is a spirit. A spirit of thought, feeling, and behavior that lives inside everyone, especially white folks—and unfortunately, Black and Brown folks also suffer from this intoxicating and violent colonization. But the spirit of whiteness primarily lives inside white bodies, which have enacted violence against Black bodies on this continent and in this country since 1619—and against the Native and Indigenous peoples of this land since arriving here—with infection, destruction, and the most fatal virus to ever infect humanity: white terrorism. Not supremacy, but sadism. Yes, I mean sadism, which means finding pleasure or excitement in inflicting pain and anguish on others (or observing such activities) without empathy. Any group of people who were empathetic, socially conscious, and humane would not have committed the atrocious crimes that white folks have committed against nonwhite folks in America.

Mere words cannot begin to capture the pain and suffering endured by Black people since being sold into enslavement centuries ago. Enslavement, torture, rape, and abuse. Mutilation, human breeding, castration, pedophilia, and sodomy. Murder, lynching, human trafficking, starvation, and intellectual theft. Degradation, dehumanization, incarceration, and spiritual and cultural destruction. These are the acts of whiteness against Black people. This is sadistic and sinister. This is racial terrorism. This is white terrorism, and there ain't nothing supreme about this behavior, nor is there anything superior about the folks who either carry it out, or who stand by and do nothing while the horror is inflicted on their fellow humans. What kind of people could do these horrendous things, be a witness to them, and/or know they are happening, yet allow them to continue for over four hundred years? White people could, and they have been doing so for centuries. But why?

There are many theories circulating about why white folks commit this kind of violence. The one I appreciate the most is the "Cress Theory," developed by Dr. Frances Cress Welsing and published in her pamphlet, *The Cress Theory of Color Confrontation and Racism (White Supremacy)*. She states that white people's minority and recessive genetic status could cause them to experience genetic annihilation. White people's population is less than ten percent of the total human population, and white skin is a recessive trait. She theorizes the collective white folks consciously and unconsciously know these truths, and they have created a set of ideas, thoughts, behaviors, and systems to compensate for their true minority status. Simply put, white folks fear genetic obliteration.

Additionally, the Cress Theory states the Black male is considered the number one threat to the white minority, because he has the power to eliminate whiteness by passing melanin down to offspring he has with white women, which can result in fewer and fewer people with white skin. Because white people (white men in particular) fear extinction, they have created an intentional strategy to attack Black men in an attempt to ensure their survival. Boom! There it is in a nutshell. Deep down inside, white folks and the white collective *know* they are a global minority and genetically inferior, and therefore they are compelled to compensate for their inferiority with so-called "white supremacy" to survive as a race. That's it. Plain and simple. And when people are desperate to survive, they will do anything, including causing the genocide of other human beings. Sounds animalistic, doesn't it? If you didn't imagine animals in the wild fighting for survival, you may have missed the point.

Here's an example. The lion has no moral compass. It has no empathy for its prey. It does not feel bad about killing other animals to survive. In fact, the lion receives great pleasure and profit from those fatal attacks that allow it to thrive. The truth is, the lion is not really the king of the jungle. It's just the most vicious and carnivorous. If all the other animals in the jungle said, "We will no longer be the lion's prey," and collectively fought back, the lion would become extinct.

And just like the fictitious zombies in the movie *Night of the Living Dead*, white folks will stop at nothing to survive. They will rob, steal, and kill to avoid becoming genetically eradicated. Violence against blackness and Black bodies is as old as time. Black folks have been traumatized by whiteness since first contact, and have experienced a tremendous amount of pain and suffering that still continue today. We can't stop talking about the pain and suffering because they have not ended. The original sin of chattel slavery has not been reconciled. There has been no atonement. No apology. No retribution or restitution. No reparations. Nothing.

As decades pass, white folks are simply returning to us what was already ours, and they are still holding on to what is due to Black people. It was never white people's place to withhold our human rights in the first place. Decency. Humanity. Empathy. Equality. Equity. Justice. Freedom and liberation.

No person or group of people should have control over these basic human rights. Yet here we are in the 21st century, still fighting, begging, pleading, marching, and protesting for what is ours to have and own without it being rationed out by white folks.

When we think about the animalistic acts of whiteness, we often envision white men as the perpetrators, but they didn't act alone. They have always had white women as co-conspirators and accomplices as they committed crimes against Black and Brown humanity. And white women have been initiators and instigators in the same violence. White women who stood silently by while white men raped, pillaged, beat, and brutalized Black bodies. White women who used the labor of Black women's bodies white disrespecting their humanity. White women who forced Black men and women into sexual encounters for their own pleasure and profit. White women who owned enslaved Africans. White women who have always been active in the degradation and dehumanization of Black people. And let's not forget, white women are also the breeders and coddlers of generations of terroristic white folks. White children have been and continue to be just as toxic and violent as their parents. What is "supreme" about this way of thinking and behaving? Nothing! That's why I don't call it "white supremacy." I call it what it is: white terrorism.

And this white terrorism has not ended. It just looks different today. I purposely reference white women a lot in this book. Because it is critical that what I call *"white woman violence"* is exposed for what it is, and that white women are also held accountable for the violence they commit. One of the hashtags I use is #WhiteWomenYourTimesUpToo, and it is.

Time's up for the Beckys and Karens of the world. We will not tolerate their violence anymore. Time's up, Barbeque Becky. Time's up, Permit Patty. And their time is especially up for how they engage with and treat Black women. White women are recklessly out of control, and white woman violence is at a peak right now.

My anti-racism work is focused not only on holding white women accountable for discovering and owning their *Weapons of Whiteness*, but also on teaching them how to disarm themselves to be less violent to Black women. Since beginning this anti-racism and racial justice work, I've been able to analyze and see into the depth and complexity of white woman violence, and it's treacherous, tenacious, and toxic.

The call to action for white women right now is to follow Black women. Instead, white women are out here collecting us—Black folks in general and Black women in particular—like Pokémon for their "See, I'm a good white woman" collection. Without blinking, they will suck our Black lives from our bodies and leave us for dead; they will spit out our bones and collect us in their skeleton graveyards behind their houses. They will wipe the blood off their lips and wander the streets looking for the next Black body to consume, use, abuse, and devour, just for their own selfish pleasure and profit. They are incessantly carnivorous. They are insatiable as they beg for emotional labor, and they are starving for cookies. They crave your Black strength and resilience, and they ravenously leech our magic. And the moment you get a whiff of their sinister and deliberate agenda, they will transform from a ravaging beast into an emotionally brittle and pathetic snowflake who disappears into the white abyss of White Silence (a Weapon of Whiteness).

There will be other white women who will become egotistically enraged that you (a Black person who they deeply despise and fear but pretend they don't) have the uppity audacity to question their sociopathology and white fake-ass pseudo-superiority. They will switch up on you faster than a transformer into a raging, righteous Becky or Karen out to destroy you. Locked and loaded with Weapons of Whiteness, they will relentlessly pursue defaming your character and putting you in your Black-ass place, Hattie and Toby. Because after all, as much as they crave your blackness, they despise it in the same sadistic breath. This is not by accident. It is by generational design.

White women are the fuel that feeds the beast (aka white terrorism) that hunts us, and they are obsessive and relentless in their pursuit and consumption of Black bodies. They never sleep, and their appetite for devouring blackness is insatiable. Unless you want to be eaten alive, you have to set barbed-wire boundaries with white folks, especially white women, and back their asses up consistently, because if you don't, they will invade your spirit and infect you with toxic whiteness.

And the truth is, this insatiable appetite for blackness and this deep, toxic, anti-blackness is in all white people. Did you hear the dichotomy in the previous sentence? Let me clarify. White folks have an unslakable appetite for the consumption of blackness, but they are also inherently anti-black. There is something sick about this truth. It is dis-eased thought. And even with this sick thought, white folks believe they are exceptional. There's no such thing as an exceptional white person.

And in my opinion, this dis-eased thought is what allows white folks to hunt for Black bodies to collect and consume. Be careful who you allow to collect you. Be careful who you befriend. Ask to see their back yard first. Trust me, you'll find the bones of Black folks who refused to bow down to white people's so-called *White Authority* (another Weapon of Whiteness). Black folks who were too bold, too unapologetic, too brave, and too courageous. Basically, Black folks who refused to be fetishized, patronized, and cannibalized. I am not exaggerating. Whiteness is virulent, violent, invasive, and lethal.

Stay woke! White people will lure you in with compliments and intoxicate you with money, favors, and resources. Believe me when I say there is always a twisted agenda, because white folks don't know how to have genuine, nonoppressive relationships with Black folks. They never thought they'd need or want to have such relationships, and they certainly have never been taught how to form and/or maintain them. Their intention is always to use you and your blackness for pleasure and profit, whether it be to tokenize and fetishize you, or to use your blackness for community clout and social capital.

Some will use you as an aphrodisiac to simply stroke their "I-am-a-good-white-person" ego. Some will slither into close proximity to gain access to your Black friends, for "friendship" or as the objects of their sexual desires. Some will take you on as their special Black charity project in an attempt to diminish their white guilt and anti-blackness. I know all this is true, because I have been used this way by every white person who has tried to befriend me. If you show me twenty random white folks who have attempted to befriend a Black person, I can find at least one way each of them is looking for some form of pleasure and profit from their relationship. I can also dig up at least one element of anti-blackness within each of those white people.

This is the truth about whiteness. And when I say, "All white people," I mean it. Even your favorites. If you push the right buttons or activate the right triggers, you will see it with your own eyes. There is nothing supreme about whiteness. Furthermore, the Weapons of Whiteness used by white people to emotionally, spiritually, and psychologically attack and harm you are real. I will be discussing some of the Weapons of Whiteness in this book, and my growing list of them is included in the Resources section. And while this book is primarily about exposing these weapons so you can identify and understand how white people use them against you, it's also about how Black people have been conditioned to wield these same weapons against each other.

It's true: we use the master's tools, aka Weapons of Whiteness, against each other, disguised as anti-blackness. The way we use these weapons to harm and destroy each other may look different from how white people use them, but the emotional, spiritual, and psychological damage is the same. We too have become so infected by toxic whiteness that even if white folks ceased to exist, we would still harm each other with the weapons they've issued us.

The indoctrination into toxic whiteness is killing us. Literally. We are fulfilling the intent of the Willie Lynch Letter with perfection, whether the letter be real or an urban legend. I say this because there are a lot of Black folks who believe the

Willie Lynch Letter is an authentic document on how to build a slave and enslave multiple generations, and others say it is a myth. A made-up artifact. For years, I thought the Willie Lynch Letter was a genuine document of strategy and instruction; however, I have since learned it may in fact be a fake. Whether it is real or not, it speaks some truth about how centuries of enslavement have resulted in generational self-hatred and anti-blackness in the Black community. I will let you decide about this infamous letter's authenticity; I have included it in this book's Resources section.

I will be sharing how we use anti-blackness as a conscious and unconscious strategy to hurt, defame, and destroy other Black people, and how these actions parallel Willie Lynch's teachings. You may already be familiar with the ways white people use toxic whiteness to harm and oppress you, but do you understand how Black people use similar tactics to harm and oppress each other? My hope in unmasking the Weapons of Whiteness disguised as anti-blackness is you will be able to develop a better understanding of how we are being used as puppets and pawns in a sick and twisted game of Black-body elimination. My hope is you will be able to see how you use anti-blackness to divide and conquer, and you will choose to stop wielding the master's tools. My hope is by reading this book, you will be able to finally rid yourself of toxic whiteness, so you can reclaim your sovereignty to be free and liberated. And finally, I hope this book offers you strategies and solutions you will be able to use not only for your own personal healing, but also for creating space and offering grace to other Black folks. This will allow all of us to heal, get free, and be liberated from our internalized toxic whiteness.

If you do not detox and disinfect yourself from whiteness, you will harm yourself and your fellow Black folks. That is the truth. I don't have all the answers, but what I share with you in this book will be a catalyst for reclaiming your sovereignty by releasing the hidden shackles of toxic whiteness so you can liberate your own life and help set the Black collective free. In this book, I share how you can live free and die trying while doing less harm to other Black folks. It's time for you to defend yourself from the Weapons of Whiteness used against you by white people, and to refuse to wield the same weapons against others in the Black community. This is our work to do—for ourselves and for each other—with accountability and love.

PLEASE TRY TO REMEMBER THAT WHAT THEY BELIEVE, AS WELL AS WHAT THEY DO AND CAUSE YOU TO ENDURE, DOES NOT TESTIFY TO YOUR INFERIORITY BUT TO THEIR INHUMANITY AND FEAR.

JAMES BALDWIN
THE FIRE NEXT TIME

CHAPTER ONE

WEAPONS OF WHITENESS

> White folks are a ticking time bomb ready to explode with toxic whiteness. All it takes is the right trigger.
>
> Catrice M. Jackson

I started using the Catriceology® phrase *"Weapons of Whiteness™"* in 2016 for a couple of reasons. First, because the insults, assaults, and invalidations that white folks inflict on Black and Brown folks are abusive and violent. Second, because any act of violence perpetrated against another human being is a form of weaponry. Even if you struggle to identify the weapons that white people use, you have almost certainly been their victim, or you have used them against other Black folks as weapons of anti-blackness. When I set out to write this book that names and defines the Weapons of Whiteness, I had two goals: to help you defend yourself from these weapons, and to help you stop using them against Black folks. Understanding the weapons is the first step toward both these goals.

Exactly what do I mean by my phrase "Weapons of Whiteness"? Weapons of Whiteness are conscious and unconscious behaviors, actions, and words used to lethally deny your existence, stifle your spirit, silence your voice, kill your joy, put you in harm's way, and paralyze your progress.

CHAPTER ONE | WEAPONS OF WHITENESS

These acts are insidious, pervasive, and invasive; they can be intentional or unintentional. For white people, wielding these weapons is as easy and unconscious as breathing. And although the use of these weapons can be subtle, you always know you've been attacked or harmed in some way. The intent behind these weapons' use is what I call the *Four D's: Deny, Defend, Derail,* and *Destroy.*

These weapons always have an intention. A purpose. A motive. A motive that may not always be conscious, but the subconscious mind discharges the weapons from a deep, dark, racist place. The intent is deadly; these weapons rooted in hostility are meant to cause psychoemotional harm. Weapons of Whiteness are abusive. Emotional abuse can be defined as "any act including confinement, isolation, verbal assault, humiliation, intimidation, infantilization, or any other treatment which may diminish the sense of identity, dignity, and self-worth." And because these Weapons of Whiteness serve to deny, defend, derail, and destroy, they also disregard and minimize your lived racial experiences, silence your voice of resistance, and blame you for the racism you experience. Never doubt the psychological mind games that white people play to harm you while denying harm was done.

Let's dive a little deeper here. The first of the Four D's is *denial.* In its simplest definition, denial is a person's strong refusal to believe, acknowledge, or accept their own or someone else's truth. You can see weapons of denial in action when Black and Brown folks talk about the racism they've experienced, and white folks refuse to believe or acknowledge the racism. Weapons of denial are self-serving and narcissistic: if white people deny *your* truth, then they don't have to face the truth of *their own* racism and anti-blackness. Using weapons of denial is a form of self-coddling for white folks; in other words, using them means white folks don't have to take responsibility for their overt racism and/or complicity with systemic racism and oppression.

Trust and believe weapons of denial are a form of manipulation, and that white folks are master manipulators. Has there ever been a time in history when they have not been? I can't name one, because it doesn't exist. Manipulation is a form of deception. The pillars of manipulation are control, confusion, distortion, and persuasion. Manipulative people will speak and act in ways that confuse and distort not only your reality, but also the truth, with the intention of maintaining control and persuading you to act or believe something for their gain. Manipulators do not have your best interests at heart. Ever. In the case of racism, white folks will discharge Weapons of Whiteness to deny your truth with tactics of manipulation to assure their comfort, control, and benefit.

Denial is deadly! It can literally kill you, both emotionally and physically. How many times have white folks denied your truth? How many times have they denied your voice or presence? How many times have they denied you access, opportunities, and resources because of the color of your skin? How many times have they denied your spouse, partner, siblings, children, friends, and ancestors? And what kind of emotional trauma has this created for you? Bouts of anger? Sleepless nights? Anxiety? Stress? High blood pressure? It's impossible to quantify the intensity, duration, and pervasiveness of this trauma over a lifetime. Yet it's real, and every day it happens to you and other Black people all over the world. And when white folks deny this trauma, they minimize or even erase it. They don't acknowledge and take responsibility for your pain; instead, they leave you wounded. That's why I refer to these types of behaviors, actions, and words as weapons!

Denial is a defensive, psychological mechanism used by all humans for one explicit reason: to create and sustain one's own safety and comfort. Denial allows you to ignore, dismiss, and/or invalidate the truth of your own pain, or the pain and suffering another person is enduring—even if (perhaps *especially* if), you are the person who caused their pain. I would argue that from a psychological perspective, denial of other people's pain is usually a selfish act of self-preservation rather than an intentional malicious attack.

I say "usually," because there are some folks who deny your truth and trauma to purposefully cause pain. These people are called "narcissists," and they know exactly what they are doing. When a narcissist denies your truth—even if it appears their denial is unintentional—it *is* a malicious act. It's hurtful as hell when someone denies your truth, especially if they are the source of your trauma. When white people deny your truth, or they dismiss or minimize your racial experiences, here's what's usually happening at a psychological (and often subconscious) level: they know racism involves white people, and they can't deal with that truth. You'll run into some who believe Black people can be racist against each other (that's not true), and/or that Black folks can be racist against white people (that's not true either).

In my experience, most white folks don't want to be considered racist. They don't believe they are racist because they are not like those horrible and blatant racists "out there." They believe themselves to not be racist because they don't see color, they believe we're all human beings, they have a Black partner or spouse, and a myriad of other reasons I'm sure you've heard in your lifetime. White folks believe they get to define what racism is and how it is played out in life. And frankly, that's some bullshit right there. It is not only narcissistic, it's dangerous. Imagine if we allowed abusers to define the word "abuse" and decide whether something is abusive or not. If we did, I can promise you there'd be significantly fewer abusers being held accountable for their heinous crimes. The same is true for white folks and racism, which is why we see racial injustice repeated daily and why racism has not ended. White folks deny the truth of your racial trauma. They define (or they think they do) racism, and then they decide what the consequences of their violence should or shouldn't be.

The problem with white folks and racism is they think other white folks are the problem. They are infected with what I call *"Intentional Projection."* In other words, they purposefully blame other white people for racism so they can project the shame and guilt of their own racism onto those other white people. Although it would behoove them to look at themselves as being part of the problem, they can't deal with the truth that they too are racist.

In fact, calling a white person a racist literally sends them into a fragile-yet-violent rage. You want to see belligerence in action? Tell a white person they are racist, and you will see a textbook, classic example of a white person gone wild! Seriously though, Intentional Projection is a form of denial. And if white folks can remain in denial about their racism and the truth of your racial experiences, they don't have to feel any ego discomfort or own up to their role in systemic and systematic racism. This is manipulation. And manipulation is emotional abuse.

All these mental gymnastics to avoid the truth are directly related to the second of the Four D's, *defend*. White people defend themselves to remain emotionally safe. It's a mind game, plain and simple. If you've ever been in any kind of relationship with someone who plays mind games, you know it's emotional trauma. This behavior is standard procedure for abusers. And you and I know there's never been a time in history when white folks have not been abusive to Black folks. Yet they will defend their innocence until they are breathless. I used to think this defense tactic was related more to white folks' need to be right, but now I'm convinced they use it as an emotional shield and regulator. White folks have a physical intolerance for discomfort. Of course they do; after all, when has there ever been a time when white folks collectively have had to be severely and consistently emotionally uncomfortable about their whiteness?

I can't think of a time, and it's certainly not happening today. Some may call this "white fragility." Although I can see why, I believe two things: one, white folks are emotionally brittle, and two, this brittleness occurs on a cellular level. And I mean literally and physically. Like it's in their DNA.

I never thought critically about this truth prior to five years ago. I had a sense there was something fundamentally wrong with white folks; after all, racism is a white folks' problem, so I knew it had to be passed on from generation to generation. But I never thought deeply about what "wrong" really meant. I'm no scientist, nor have I conducted any formal research, but I've been noticing this cellular response from white women in particular over the last several years. And what I've observed happens like clockwork in every city where I have hosted a workshop for white women. They are fundamentally the same no matter where I go. Different names and faces, but the Weapons of Whiteness are always reflexively launched.

Have you ever heard of WWBS, or Wimpy White Boy Syndrome? It's a nursing term often used in the NICU (Neonatal Intensive Care Unit) for premature white male babies. Also known as White Boy Syndrome, WWBS postulates that white male babies who are born prematurely are the weakest of the preemies; they languish and take longer to develop. In contrast, Black girls are the strongest, and they are the most likely to thrive in the NICU despite receiving inadequate healthcare due to racism. Although there is no extensive or conclusive research available indicating why this is true about white males, statistically white male frailty among premature babies is a real thing. And one thing is clear: gender and race are predominant factors. After all, all male preemies, regardless of skin color, fare less well in the NICU than female preemies do. Doesn't sound like any kind of supremacy to me!

While travelling over the past five years, I have been paying special attention to how this fragility or brittleness shows up in white kids. In the public spaces I move through, it's most often white kids who are ranting, screaming, pouting, running recklessly, and throwing tantrums. Next time you're on a plane, notice how many white babies are screaming. When shopping, notice how it's white kids who are running through the store, and how they touch everything in sight with few or no consequences. When out and about, notice how it's white kids who are getting smart and disrespecting their parents. Have you witnessed these same behaviors? It seems like white children are always whining, crying, and acting a fool! I mean, what do the most "privileged" children in the world have to cry and whine about? Not a damn thing!

You can witness this fragility in the media also. From the early days of silent movies, white women have been crying and throwing exaggerated emotional tantrums. They've been damsels in distress since forever, and white men always defend them and come to their rescue. As the tears roll down those white women's faces, the fuse is lit for a violent bomb to go off. White men will take care of whoever caused those white women to cry in an explosion of retaliation. In Westerns, many saloon brawls were about white men "getting even" with someone for causing a white woman to cry. The husbands, fathers, and sons of those white women defy the Wimpy White Boy Syndrome within and launch into fist fights with the offenders. The police are called and investigations are launched, all because of a white woman's tears. These are not tears of sorrow, but rather dog whistles that summon a lynch mob, or at a minimum, a RoboCop ready to defend these dangerous damsels in distress. White tears are deliberate and fatal.

Not only are white women's tears deliberate and lethal defense mechanisms, they are also acts of *derailment*, the third of the Four D's. Talking about racism for white people is like standing in the middle of a raging fire they can't escape. I think it's one of the most excruciating and dreadful experiences they encounter, especially for a white person who thinks they are one of the good ones and/or who has yet to begin the work of uprooting their racism.

I remember an incident that happened one time when I was in the grocery store with my elderly mother. There was a white woman in the checkout lane behind us (I'll call her Walmart Wendy) who was irritated because we required two separate transactions. (My mother is disabled and lives on a fixed income, so she does her shopping once a month and always buys a lot at that time.) Walmart Wendy was becoming more annoyed by the minute. She began slamming her grocery items on the checkout belt with a "hurry up and get out of my way" attitude. In between each slammed item, she expelled deep sighs of frustration and glared at me with disgust. At one point, she reached so far over my mother's shoulder (who was sitting in the electric shopping cart), that she brushed up against my mother's back. I had been trying to ignore her, but once she violated my mother's physical space, I'd had it.

I said to Walmart Wendy, "Don't you ever invade my mother's space or touch her." I told her to back the f*ck up, and I called her a racist. I could see the rage in her pasty face. She became engulfed in flames as she stood there looking as horrified as if I had told her she was going to die. Paralyzed in place with her mouth hanging open, she was infuriated by me calling her a racist. She was temporarily so undone she couldn't move. But that didn't last long. Deadly tears began to well up in her eyes. She said, "How dare you call me a racist! You're the one who is racist."

After a short exchange of heated words, Walmart Wendy furiously snatched her items off the checkout belt and threw them into her shopping cart. Becky, was she pissed! So damn mad that she started crying and declaring how it was my fault, and she was going to report me to the store manager. And she did. Ultimately, I didn't care if she reported me to security or the manager, because we had done nothing wrong. But I also knew how deadly white women's tears are, and I was concerned for my mother's and my safety. By the time we were finished checking out, Walmart Wendy had found the store manager and told him her side of the story, which of course was all white lies and dog whistles. That's what white folks do.

As my mother and I were leaving the store, the store manager asked us what happened. I told him the truth. Walmart Wendy was standing next to him, and as expected, she denied her aggressive and disrespectful acts. When she realized the store manager wasn't reprimanding me like she wanted him to, she began crying, stomped out of the store, and declared she would never shop there again! Her manipulative, violent, and toxic white tears didn't work for her in this case, which enraged her even more. If they had worked, it's likely my mother and I would have been either unfairly (and possibly violently) escorted out of the store, or the police would have been called. And you know what can happen when the police are called on Black people. Being called a racist was probably one of the most horrifying experiences Walmart Wendy had ever had, and I bet she was devastated and seething for the rest of the day. Because how dare I, an inferior Black woman (in her mind), have the damn audacity to call her a racist? After all, I'm sure she believes she's one of the *good* ones.

Walmart Wendy's tears served several purposes. First, they were a clear indication of her emotional inability (and unwillingness) to face her racism and tolerate my pointing it out (emotional brittleness). Second, they were manipulative; she hoped her tears would convince the store manager to do her dirty work and put us Black people in our place. And third, they were strategically and deliberately used to derail the violent issue at hand, her racist behavior.

White folks are experts at derailment, especially when it comes to talking about racism or being confronted about their racism, which they seem to equate with death itself. They will go to unimaginable extremes to avoid feeling the discomfort of being called out on their racism. And their acts of derailment come in all shapes and sizes. I'm sure you've been derailed by white people, even if you didn't know what to call this weaponized behavior. So why do they do this? And why do I call it a weapon? I could literally write an entire book just on derailment, but instead I'll share some common examples of how it's used and sprinkle more throughout this book.

So, returning to Walmart Wendy. At one point during our exchange, she angrily declared I was the one who was racist. Yeah, she tried it. She pulled out the classic comeback white people use when you call them a racist and/or point out their racist behavior. She pulled out the reverse racism card. Yawn. It's a classic one, isn't it? So damn predictable and unoriginal. Not to mention, there's no such thing as reverse racism. We know this, but it seems white folks have not yet figured out this laughable comeback is both erroneous and funny as hell when you really think about how ridiculous it is. For reals. When I get this response from white folks, I either laugh out loud, or if I'm on social media, I use the laughing emoji (which irritates them even more). And then I simply stop talking and walk away.

Because when you get the reverse racism response from white folks, you already know you're dealing with

CHAPTER ONE | WEAPONS OF WHITENESS

Whitepeopling 101. These folks are literally starting from scratch on their anti-racism journey, and they are also committed to willful ignorance. They don't want to learn. They don't want to change. Above all, they want to be right, and they feel entitled to their righteousness. And when folks are committed to being right at all costs, it truly is a waste of your time and life source. Walk away! Don't give them a drop of your emotional labor. And mind you, this claim of reverse racism is a tactic used to derail the conversation about racism. White people want to shift the focus off their racism in particular. Their denial becomes a weapon.

One of the most annoying Weapons of Whiteness white folks wield is *White Interrogation*. And yup, it's exactly what you think it is: when white folks ask a thousand irritating, stupid, and gaslighting questions! And trust me, they are not just random questions of curiosity. They are deliberate and loaded with motives, and they are intended to derail the conversation about racism. And not just to derail it, but also to avoid personal accountability, to emotionally exhaust you, and to shut down the conversation. In other words, they will question you to death! Questions such as:

- *"Why do you always focus on and talk about race?"*
- *"Do you think Black people can be racist too?"*
- *"Do you think there are any good white folks?"*
- *"Don't you think capitalism is a bigger issue than racism?"*
- *"Well, what should white people do to end racism?"*

Blah. Blah. Blah...Blah...Blah! I'm sure you've heard these questions or others like them from white people hundreds of times. And the questions are not original. They come straight from the white folks' script they have mastered and recited from their entire lives. I know you've seen criminal suspects being interrogated into submission on television, right? Well, in this case, you are the suspect, and if you start answering these manipulative questions, you will submit to being stirred into the Sunken Place. You will become emotionally drained and psychologically exhausted. Which are the intentions of the questions, after all: White Interrogation's sole purpose is to emotionally suck the life out of you so you don't have the emotional or mental energy to stay focused on the real issue, which is white folks' racism. The goal is to take you down a rabbit hole, so you'll forget about the racist behavior they demonstrated toward you. Don't fall for the okie doke!

The last example of derailment I want to talk about in this chapter is when white folks insist capitalism is the reason for racism. When white folks pull out this weapon, they are essentially saying, "Looking at my whiteness and how it has harmed others and benefited me is uncomfortable, so let me deflect with a 'capitalism is worse than racism' comment." The intention is to seek a strategic alliance with you centered around the rich versus the poor to trick you into shifting your focus. And if you're not part of the "elite and rich" crowd, you may just fall victim to this weaponized, manipulative tactic. White folks love to derail conversations about race and racism by injecting comments about how capitalism is worse than racism.

Let's first tackle the deception in these ideas. For context I'll be referring to racism and capitalism as they exist in the United States. The derailment tactic of "capitalism is worse than racism," or the pressure for you to focus on capitalism as the root of all our social ills, is fundamentally a lie. Does capitalism merit attention and dismantling? Of course it does. Does capitalism exacerbate racism? Absolutely. But don't get it twisted. Poor white folks are racist too.

And let's not forget how whiteness lethally and illegally seized native lands from the Indigenous peoples while raping their women, killing their leaders, and kidnapping their children to ship them off to abusive boarding schools. Well, let's tell the damn truth about those so-called "schools." The children were beaten, abused, and tortured with the intention of "beating the savage" out of them. Who did this to these children? White women! White women who today love to deny their legacy of violence and barbarism. Don't ever think white women weren't participants in the violence against Black and Brown bodies. Thousands upon thousands of native children of this land we call America were mercilessly ripped from their parents' arms and forced to conform and assimilate into white expectations. It was white women who shamed, beat, brutalized, and punished these helpless children into submission. White woman violence is not new. Their violent tendencies are as potent and virulent as those of the white men they despise, bow down to, and hide behind for protection.

White historians may tell their stories of lies about why the white colonizers damn near annihilated the Indigenous peoples of this land. They may paint a pretty picture of the colonizers' legacy of destruction, corruption, and genocide to make themselves feel better. But one thing is clear: the white colonizers did these inhumane things to the native peoples because those people were not white.

The white colonizers perceived the Indigenous peoples to be inferior savages who needed to be conquered and destroyed. Even before the term "race" was created by white people, this crusade to literally wipe out an entire group of people was racism. The European colonizers' racism allowed them to take native lands for capitalistic gain. And their greedy and grotesque behaviors continued when they carried out one of the world's largest and lethal crimes against Black bodies in history based on a fake-ass and false social construct of race. A construct today they hate to admit they created and don't want to be critiqued or called out on. In the U.S., there would be no capitalism as we know it today without the vile and violent acts of racism and anti-blackness committed by European colonizers and their diabolical descendants.

Is capitalism the cause of racism in America? It is not the cause, but instead a byproduct of racism revealed by colonization, theft, genocide, and the inhumane acts of buying, selling, enslaving, and brutalizing African people for centuries. Now let me be clear. Capitalism is definitely a motive here. America's wealth was barbarically built on the backs of enslaved Africans, Black people. Ruthlessness, violence, and inhumanity were motives for sure, as were the forced indoctrination of hypocritical Christianity and the raping of tribal culture. Would the U.S. have established itself as an economic leader and powerhouse without racism and corrupt religion? According to Matthew Desmond, the answer is clearly no:

> Slavery was undeniably a font of phenomenal wealth. By the eve of the Civil War, the Mississippi Valley was

home to more millionaires per capita than anywhere else in the United States. Cotton grown and picked by enslaved workers was the nation's most valuable export. The combined value of enslaved people exceeded that of all the railroads and factories in the nation. New Orleans boasted a denser concentration of banking capital than New York City. What made the cotton economy boom in the United States, and not in all the far-flung parts of the world with climates and soil suitable to the crop, was our nation's unflinching willingness to use violence on nonwhite people and to exert its will on seemingly endless supplies of land and labor. Given the choice between modernity and barbarism, prosperity and poverty, lawfulness and cruelty, democracy and totalitarianism, America chose all of the above.

—Matthew Desmond, "If you want to understand the brutality of American capitalism, you have to start on the plantation," *The New York Times Magazine: The 1619 Project,* August 14, 2019

The U.S. economy would be absolutely nothing without stolen land and Black bodies. The unlawful seizure of land and the uncivilized and barbaric Trans-Atlantic Slave Trade are the true and ugly roots of American wealth and American capitalism.

So, for all those folks who choose to derail conversations about racism in the United States with this tactic of focusing on capitalism instead, they need to stop it. Because it's just that: a strategic tactic to dismiss the racist and violent nature of white folks so they can avoid the discomfort of facing the truth about these original sins and their role as the deadly and diabolical roots of capitalism. And until this vile root is plucked from these stolen lands that are soaked with Black and Indigenous blood, the fruits of this country will always be bitter and rotten. Black people, descendants of enslaved Africans, know this truth. Stand on this truth unwaveringly, and do not allow the lies to deceive you. For derailment, which is an act of violence, is surely a weapon used against you and one you may be using against other Black people. I hope you lay down this Weapon of Whiteness, for it is just one of the master's tools.

The last-but-not-least of the Four D's is *destroy*. When white people use Weapons of Whiteness, their intention is to destroy Black and Brown (nonwhite) people spiritually, psychologically, and emotionally. This destruction can look like silencing you, trying to make you feel crazy, and/or serving as a catalyst for your literal death. Weapons of Whiteness are like bullets in a gun. They aim to wound and kill. And they do. These weapons destroy your peace, destroy your reputation and credibility, destroy your careers and jobs, and destroy your sense of safety and right to exist in your Black body. And when white folks wield their weapons, you can die, and there is a long list of hashtags leaving a trail of blood from the carnage.

It should not come as a surprise that Weapons of Whiteness are destructive, because as I say, there has never been a time in history when whiteness has not been violent. There has never been a time in the history of the United States when nonwhite people have been treated with dignity and respect. There has never been a time in this country when

Black folks have not been demoralized, dehumanized, and destroyed in some way. In fact, has there ever been a time when the collective white folks have treated any group of nonwhite folks lovingly and humanely? Nope. Never.

Whiteness in these here United States has always been violent and destructive to Black and Brown bodies. White supremacy is a myth. A straight-up lie. A damn delusion. There is absolutely nothing "supreme" about the folks who have raped, murdered, lynched, and brutalized nonwhite bodies since the first day they arrived on this stolen land. White folks have willfully wielded their Weapons of Whiteness to cause mass destruction on Black bodies yesterday, today, and for every tomorrow that comes. This is not by accident. It's by design and with ill intent. Weapons of Whiteness are the true menaces to society, enacted to steal, kill, and destroy. Some people say white folks have lost their humanity. My response to that statement is a question: "Did they ever have it to lose?"

LAY DOWN YOUR WEAPONS

WHITE TEARS: When white folks cry during discussions about racism, and/or claim they feel attacked, shamed, and hurt when their racism is pointed out or confronted.

When you are confronted about your racism, or your anti-black behavior is pointed out, how have you used tears to deflect your anti-blackness and/or to shift the blame?

_____

_____

_____

_____

WHITE INTERROGATION: When white folks ask Black and Brown folks too many emotionally laborious DAMN questions, often as a derailment tactic.

When trying to understand the reality of someone lighter or darker than you, have you exhausted them with a thousand questions?

_____

_____

_____

_____

> TO BE A NEGRO IN THIS COUNTRY AND TO BE RELATIVELY CONSCIOUS IS TO BE IN A RAGE ALMOST ALL THE TIME.
>
> JAMES BALDWIN

CHAPTER
TWO

WEAPONRY 101
THE WEAPON FORMERLY KNOWN AS FRAGILITY

White people are not fragile. They are violent as hell.

Catrice M. Jackson

In the hundreds of years since landing on indigenous soil in the United States, white folks have done nothing but conquer, kill, lie, steal, and bulldoze their way over Black and Brown bodies to seize land, lives, resources, and access. Where's the lie? I'll wait. We still see it today in mass incarceration of Black bodies, gentrification, and police brutality, to name just a few acts of white terrorism. Some historians say white folks had to convince themselves Black people were NOT human in order to carry out their atrocities against Black bodies. Not just once or twice, but for almost three centuries of chattel slavery and decades of discriminatory and racist violence thereafter. They saw Black people as unhuman (meaning "not resembling or having the qualities of a human being") and treated them no better than farm animals and dogs. This is the sick justification you'll hear from many white writers about the horrific crimes committed against Black bodies during slavery.

These acts of violence were deliberate, not accidental. Whenever I hear this pitiful, gaslighting justification white people use about their ancestors' actions, I laugh inside. Not because it's funny, but because it is crystal clear who was actually unhuman (and *inhuman*, meaning "lacking human qualities of compassion and mercy; cruel and barbaric") in order to behave in such horrific, animalistic ways. More importantly, what kind of wretched people consciously and willingly have sex with animals, with the "unhumans" they deemed the lowest of the low? I mean, really, take a minute to dissect that diabolical cognitive dissonance.

You might be surprised to hear how many times I've received this justification to my question of, "If Black people, enslaved Africans, were *not* human, and were seen as savages and animals, then why did so many white women and men rape, sodomize, and have sex with them?" My follow-up question is always, "So, is this part of white European culture— to have sex with animals, to engage in bestiality?" Most white folks, primarily white women, quickly and emphatically deny these acts of sexual "perversion" as part of white European culture. Their culture. And of course, my response is always, "Then explain to me how this was a legal, constant occurrence for almost three hundred years if it is not part of white culture." Their white faces answer me by adopting vacant, confused, and seethingly angry expressions. They do not know how to respond to these logical and fact-based questions. Most times, they sit paralyzed and puzzled, and some become red and angry.

I think these are legitimate questions, don't you? They are. But what's really happening here is not your classic case of cognitive dissonance. It's a flat-out lie. A heinous one. White folks who spew this lie are simply justifying the monstrous acts committed against Black bodies. Black people. Black human beings. And just like silence is violence, denial is violence too.

The denial of it all, and the desperate attempts to erase the truth about what Black people endured (and are enduring) from whiteness, is just as sadistic as the acts themselves. White folks have been relentlessly, recklessly, and unapologetically discharging these Weapons of Whiteness since the existence of white folks. Like forever. But why? I mean, really. What is the source of all this violence and destruction? What makes the collective white people cause so much harm to Black folks, and also to themselves? After all, most of them are clueless about the harm centuries of white violence has also done to white folks. Boy, do I wish I had an undisputed answer to these questions. However, I do have a few theories and truths that might make sense to you.

Early in my journey of becoming a social and racial justice advocate, activist, and educator, I naively believed white folks were broken and fragile. I also believed the false narrative that not *all* white people are racist. And I believed racism was primarily a learned behavior and white folks just needed to do better. Essentially, what I believed about white folks and their racism is what white folks wanted me to believe. And I believed it because I too was indoctrinated by whiteness to not know any better. I didn't fully realize just how much I'd been infected by it. And still am.

Can you relate to this? Or have you always believed something different from this? I think if you're honest, you too might have once believed (and maybe still do) that not all white people are racist, they just need to learn how to not be racist.

If so, there's no shame in that, but I guarantee you whiteness taught you your beliefs. This is what Brother Malcolm is talking about when he says, "Who taught you to...?" You might be thinking Black folks also taught you these things, and you'd be correct. But who taught them? And who taught those teachers? We can keep tracing these false teachings back generation after generation, and we'll arrive at the original teachers: white folks! These lessons came straight from the plantation masterclass and were enforced with one of the oldest tricks in the white supremacy book, which is to use the manipulation of Black folks to manipulate Black folks. This was a true black-on-black crime committed against Black folks over and over again. They taught us to hate us. And we've been passing down this plantation education for generations, to our own detriment and destruction.

For years I had heard the term "woke" used by Black folks, but I didn't really know what it meant. I remember watching Spike Lee's *School Daze* when it debuted in 1988. I was in my late teens, and I was mostly getting it, but not fully. With so many layers of messaging in the movie, my young brain was not able to take them all in and metabolize them for self-empowerment. One of the most profound scenes was when Spike's character, Half-Pint, screamed "Wake up," and then other characters followed suit. I can vividly remember the scene, and today the words "wake up" have so much more meaning, depth, and power for me. In more ways than I can count, I was so asleep back then—and if I'm honest, I was still sleeping quite a bit just five years ago, but I was waking up more and more each day.

But my real wake-up call happened in February 2012.

And like the soul-stirring moment in *School Daze*, this moment, my true wake-up call, is still hauntingly vivid today. Two words describe it best: Trayvon Martin. Gunned down and murdered in cold blood. Simply for being Black and minding his own business. Killed by a cowardly predator named George Zimmerman. A grown-ass man, wanna-be cop consumed by anti-blackness. On that sobering day of February 26th, 2012, a piece of my heart died too. I was instantly devastated and in shock that someone could literally follow a Black kid for no justifiable reason and then shoot him dead. I know that sounds unrealistic given this type of violence has been happening toward Black folks since we were unwillingly brought to this country. I knew it was possible because of the overwhelming evidence of white violence that has been perpetrated and well-documented for centuries. But if I'm being transparent and honest, the real reason it hit me so hard and registered deep within my soul was because in Trayvon's murder, I could clearly see my own son's mortality for the first time. My son, my only child, turned twenty that same year.

Sadly, but also thankfully, sometimes events have to hit home before we truly see the problems and challenges other people are facing, and then we wake up! Often, social and racial injustice has to knock on our own door for us to give a damn. I knew without a doubt Black boys, men, women, and girls had been hunted and gunned down just like Trayvon was, but that knowledge hadn't touched me deeply until it affected me personally. That sounds horrible and insensitive, but it's true.

I believe another reason I was hit so hard by Trayvon's tragic death was because I was away from my nineteen-year-old son for the first time in his life. I was living in Dallas, Texas at the time, and my son was living in another state with my mother. I had relocated to Texas with the hope that my son would be joining my husband and me there, but after a month, my son told me he did not want to move to Texas. We had never been apart from each other, and the distance between us was already taking an emotional toll on me. I was feeling raw and guilty, because I believed children are supposed to leave their parents, not the other way around. It just didn't feel right to not have my son in Texas with us.

As the Trayvon Martin murder and investigation played out in the media, and as public awareness was growing about the case, I was consumed with fear of what could happen to my own son just for existing in Black skin and walking around in a specific kind of sweatshirt. A hoodie. I recall many moments when I would break down and cry thinking about what had happened to Trayvon, and I would envision my son's face inside a hoodie. The anger, fear, and grief were unbearable. This was my wake-up call. I knew I had to do something to be part of the solution. And over the first three weeks of the Trayvon Martin ordeal, God was clearly speaking to me. Several times during this horrific time, I heard God's voice say, "This is it. This is your calling. It's time for you to say yes and take action." Even now, tears are running down my face as I write this. It's as if I am in that moment of awakening for the first time again. And while all Black lives that have been stolen matter, the mention of Trayvon's name still makes me tearful today. I will never forget Trayvon. His life still matters. Black lives do matter.

Although Trayvon's murder shook me to my core and broke me down, it also ignited a fire in my soul. A fire for truth, racial justice, and Black freedom and liberation. Three more years passed before I finally took tangible action to be obedient to God's call. The whispers from the divine were not only consistent and profound during this period, they often kept me up at night and in constant prayer for Black men and boys all over the country. Including my son.

Finally, in March 2015, I said yes to God's call. I walked away from the branding and marketing coaching work I was doing at the time. It was okay work, and I was excellent at it, but it sure wasn't feeding my soul. Trayvon's murder and my own personal awakening to what is really happening to Black folks in America served as the catalyst for what I call *"The Awakened Conscious Shift."* While I believe this awakening of consciousness, and this shift in behavior required by all humanity, is critical to making life less oppressive for Black folks in particular, it is not the core reason for the work I do today. Yes, it's important for us to wake up to the atrocities faced by Black folks, and yes, we must shift the way we see and treat each other, but racial justice and Black liberation are the pillars of the work I've been called to do. Period.

Let's step back to how this chapter began. White lies. White denial. White destruction and white violence. I am no longer naive about the violence of whiteness and the harm white folks are capable of inflicting on humanity. I am not confused at all about why they have been traumatizing Black bodies generation after generation. These truths about the collective white folks, about whiteness, are not made-up exaggerations. I'm not imagining these horrendous acts. And I sure as hell ain't losing my mind about the reality of it all. And you are not confused, exaggerating, imagining it, or losing your mind either.

Man... Black folks have been through hell and back in the United States. And we are still in the middle of the fire. Fighting for our lives and humanity in one way or another every single day. Even those of us who think we have somehow escaped the trap through upward mobility, access, opportunity, and wealth still cannot escape our blackness and the barrage of offenses committed against Black bodies. I'm also extremely clear about how we Black folks survive and sometimes thrive in the face of this ominous oppression day in and day out, yet white folks cannot (and often will not) even engage in and/or emotionally tolerate a conversation about racism and collective white violence. In other words, they engage in "white fragility."

This so-called frailty is a fraud. It's an outright lie. It is a manipulative scam. The phrase "white fragility" was coined by Robin DiAngelo, a white woman. You can read about her theory and development of the phrase. I am not going to give her any airtime other than to acknowledge her ties to the phrase. Why? Because she simply regurgitates facts about racism and white terrorism she's learned from Black people. She ain't brand new, and nothing she talks about isn't anything Black folks don't already know.

In fact, I won't spend much time talking about white fragility as DiAngelo theorizes it; instead, I'll state it is one of the top five weapons used by white folks to deny their racism, minimize their racist behaviors, and emotionally bully you into shutting the hell up so they can turn the tables and become the victim in all situations where racism is the topic of discussion. It is one of the most manipulative, strategic, and pitiful weapons white folks use. I mean, seriously, they don't have the emotional fortitude, psychological capability, or resiliency to even *talk* about racism? Get the f*ck out of here!

The word I use to describe white folks' inability and unwillingness to confront their racism and engage in conversations about racism is "pathetic." Calling white folks racist seems like the absolute worst thing you can do to them. As Walmart Wendy demonstrated in Chapter 1, they really lose their shit and become defensive, discombobulated, and often psychologically and emotionally deadly. White folks' frailty has gotten Black folks killed, lynched, arrested, falsely accused, and incarcerated, and their lack of empathy for Black bodies causes Black people to get written up, suspended, and fired from jobs.

What's fragile about that violence? It's not fragile; it's ferocious. It's like asking a pedophile to talk about child sexual abuse, and that causes them to become so distraught they can't function, yet they have enough emotional capacity to hunt, kidnap, and rape children. Does that make sense to you? Nah! I don't buy it. White folks just do not want to talk about their racism and complicity in the racial crimes committed against Black bodies. It's that simple. And it is pathetic. It's particularly pathetic when the white collective consciously and unconsciously believes they are superior to Black and Brown folks, especially Black folks. Like seriously. How can someone be superior when they have the emotional intelligence and fortitude of a toddler?

As far as I'm concerned, the word "fragility" needs to be replaced with the word "manipulation." Because if we examine this fragility closer, there is absolutely nothing frail about it. Underneath this façade is a tool, a mechanism that is deceitful, deliberate, and destructive. A mechanism that causes significant emotional harm to Black folks. Harm in the form of an abusive and narcissistic mind control or a dangerous dog whistle that is the prelude to violence being committed against Black bodies.

Let me explain. Think back to an encounter you've had with a white person where they behaved in a racist way toward you. A time when you pointed out their racist behavior and/or called them out on their violence. A time when they cried or alleged you were shaming them. What did they say? What was their facial expression? How did they behave? Let me guess. They more often than not turned red in the face and neck. Their facial expression was one of shock and confusion, with elements of seething anger or outright pissed-offedness. And they probably said things like, "How dare you call me racist," or, "You don't know me, I don't have a racist bone in my body." Or perhaps the classic textbook response of, "I don't care whether people are black, brown, purple, or green!" And if they were really performing for the Academy Awards, white tears flooded their face. Sounds about right.

How did I know this? Because these are learned responses—taught to white people by their families, friends, and the white supremacy culture—and they are innate actions of white manipulation (aka white fragility). These responses have the Four D's I described in Chapter 1 as their intentions: they are intended to *deny* white people's racism, *defend* their white innocence, *derail* any further conversation about their racism, and *destroy* the truth about their violence and your lived racial experiences.

This, my friend, is a manipulative mind game. And it is still a mind f*ck whether they do it intentionally or unintentionally. It doesn't matter if it is purposeful or not. What matters is this violent act of racism happened, and harm was done. Period. This is what I mean by *abusive and narcissistic mind control*. Because if the performance is played out correctly, it will cause you to re-think what just happened to you. The tears may cause you to feel sorry for your abuser. You may begin to second-guess your response to their racism. And when this psychological trick works as designed, you'll end up thinking you're the one in the wrong. You will become convinced you are the aggressor!

The inability to engage in real conversations about racism without becoming emotionally discombobulated, lashing out, and/or withdrawing. This is my definition of this so-called white fragility. Sounds like fragility, but psychologically speaking, it's not. What lurks beneath this vicious veneer is something far more white "supremacist" than you might imagine. When white folks become frail during conversations about racism, and/or when they are called out on their racism, it's not fragility, it's seething rage! It's white rage. And if you look several layers below the surface frailty, you will see two Weapons of Whiteness at work.

First, you will see the weapon of *White Entitlement*. This is when white folks believe they are entitled to consume time, space, and conversations in order to be the center of attention, and when they expect to be taught, considered, and forgiven. It is also when white folks believe they have the God-given right to observe, analyze, critique, abuse, attack, and consume Black bodies. In other words, white people believe they have the right to be racist, the right to act racist, and the right to attack blackness because they deem themselves superior to Black people.

This pseudo-superiority leads me to the second Weapon of Whiteness that lurks beneath white people's toddler-esque frailty: *White Authority*. This is when white folks use their whiteness to dominate folks of color: speaking for and over, interrupting, taking up space, cutting in line, and dismissing their presence. White Authority is when white folks believe they make the rules, call the shots, and control the narrative in every way and in every space. White folks' racist acts all stem from this one violent weapon. They believe they have the right to do and say whatever the hell they want with no consequences, critiques, or callouts.

And when Black folks have the nerve to call out white folks on their shit, the weapons of White Entitlement and White Authority are launched in a child-like way, resulting in white tears and the weapon formerly known as fragility. When white folks are called racist and/or their racist acts are confronted, they get pissed as hell that you would question and tamper with their right and entitlement over your inferior Black self. How dare you challenge their authority to know what is racist and what's not. How dare you step out of line and behave like one of those uppity negroes. How dare you get out of the oppressive box they expect you to die in, and how dare you use that kind of tone and audacity to your superiors! Yup! All that is happening in the quick moments that pass by when you confront their violence and toxic whiteness.

What you once knew as fragility is fundamentally histrionics! Academy Award-winning performances are what you see when white folks are confronted with their racism. Histrionics are overly dramatic responses and exaggerated melodramatics designed to get attention; they are one big, vehement act of centering. In other words, they are unjustifiably extra! I mean, seriously, think about it. When you envision someone being frail or fragile, does the way white folks respond to racial stress look fragile? When they lash out and retaliate, is that soft, delicate, and weak? When they try to get you written up or fired, is that passive? When they call the police on you for not tolerating their bullshit, is that docile? Nah! Every response you experience is spiteful, treacherous, and volatile.

They ain't fragile. They are master manipulators. Especially white women. Do not believe this lie. They are ticking time bombs that will explode, maim, and kill at any moment. Let's stop believing and perpetuating this great white lie of fragility! And isn't it ironic that the phrase "white fragility" was created by a white person? How conveniently coddling is that? It's like a rattlesnake saying, "I'm harmless," while their deadly tail rattles. Even when white folks attempt to be a voice against racism, there is violence in their "do-gooder" performative acts. Don't listen to the harmless hiss. The rattle tells you who you are really dealing with.

LAY DOWN YOUR WEAPONS

WHITE FRAGILITY: When white folks are unable to engage in real conversations about racism without becoming emotionally discombobulated, lashing out, and/or withdrawing.

When you are confronted about your racism, or your anti-black behavior is pointed out, how have you withdrawn, become brittle, or lashed out at Black folks?

_____

_____

_____

_____

WHITE DENIAL: When white folks refuse to admit to their racism and/or to acknowledge the systemic and structural racism and oppression of white terrorism.

How do you respond to accusations of anti-blackness or colorism?

_____

_____

_____

_____

AS WHITE WOMEN IGNORE THEIR BUILT-IN PRIVILEGE OF WHITENESS AND DEFINE WOMAN IN TERMS OF THEIR OWN EXPERIENCE ALONE, THEN WOMEN OF COLOR BECOME "OTHER," THE OUTSIDER WHOSE EXPERIENCE AND TRADITION IS TOO "ALIEN" TO COMPREHEND.

AUDRE LORDE
SISTER OUTSIDER: ESSAYS AND SPEECHES

CHAPTER THREE

WHITE WOMAN VIOLENCE 101

> White women are the fuel that feeds the beast of white terrorism that hunts us. They are the neck, and the head can't move or survive without the neck.
>
> Catrice M. Jackson

If I could sit down right now and commune with my great-grandmother and my great-great-grandmother, I am one hundred percent sure they would tell me horror stories about how white folks treated them. And I am certain they would tell monstrous stories about white women too.

The intentional white washing of white women's roles in the savagery committed against Black bodies in this country is, as my mama would say, a bald-faced lie. Complete erasure of white women's cellular capacity to steal, kill, and destroy. To steal babies. To kill Black folks or be the cause of their death. To destroy Black lives and families. And they didn't just have the capacity for the horrific acts they perpetrated against Black bodies, they actually carried out those acts, even though this history is rarely talked about. White woman violence is not only ancient, it is also contemporary. And it has always been nefarious.

My late grandmother, who passed away in 2010, didn't talk much about her mother, my great-grandmother Rachel, except for her stories about how horribly Rachel was treated by white folks. And according to my grandmother, my great-grandmother was a slave. My grandmother would sometimes talk about how she remembers walking in the fields with her mother as she picked cotton. As a young girl and woman, I did not fully understand the depravity of what she described. I also didn't ask the questions I wish I could ask today to get a better understanding of my grandmother and great-grandmother's experiences dealing with toxic whiteness and white woman violence. I wish my grandmother were still alive, not only to learn more about the violence and trauma she and her elders experienced back in the day, but also to affirm I get it better and deeper than I ever have before.

White women have been violent since their first encounters with Black folks centuries ago. This chapter highlights the distinctive violence white women enact; however, all white folks are armed with Weapons of Whiteness. Can you think of a time when white women have not caused direct or indirect harm against you, your parents, grandparents, or your great-grandparents? They have been terrorizing Black bodies for at least four generations, and I believe it's been even longer. Since forever.

Using the word "violence" to describe the complacency, complicity, and co-conspiracy of white women's roles in the dehumanization and brutalization of Black bodies is a gross understatement. It only scratches the sinister surface of the dehumanizing disdain white women have for Black lives. Yet "violence" is the word I use for two reasons. First, because white women's actions, or lack thereof, have directly and indirectly caused emotional, psychological, and physical harm to Black people. Second, the word "violence" startles white women, grabs their attention, and points out clearly and undeniably the role they play in white terrorism. And yes, "terrorism" is the correct term. There is nothing supreme about the brutality, inhumanity, and violence of whiteness. Tell me a time in American history, including now, when white folks have not been collectively violent toward Black folks, and I will consider a new word.

When I finally decided to answer the calling for my life to be a racial justice advocate, educator, and activist, and I began to speak out against white supremacy (aka white terrorism), racism, and anti-blackness, I committed to doing so with clarity, conviction, and with a straight-up, no-chaser style. I refuse to sugarcoat the truth and coddle white folks while Black people are dying every day due to systemic and systematic racism. I deliberately choose explicit words to speak about this terror, and I am candid in my conversations about it. Because there has never been a time in American history when white folks have not terrorized Black people.

And because Black bodies continue to be dehumanized and brutalized, there is no time to waste on dancing around the issues and glossing over the truth. Not just the truth, the radical truth. Truth that hurts. Truth that penetrates. Truth that causes a visceral reaction. Truth that causes white folks to take immediate and direct action about their own violence and the violence of their fellow white folks. So, I choose to use the word "violence" to illustrate the complicity, complacency, and racially motivated actions of white women.

In fact, the behaviors of white women, whether conscious or unconscious, are reminiscent of the textbook definition of the phrase "psychological abuse." This abuse does not discriminate. It doesn't matter what type of relationship you are in with white women or whether you know them intimately or not. There is a long list of narcissistic behaviors used by emotional or psychological abusers to cause harm; here are just a few: threats, name calling, emotional outbursts, false accusations, blame, denial, gaslighting, trivializing, dehumanizing, interrupting, and turning others against you. The use of any combination of these tactics causes psychological harm to the recipient. And often the harm leads to trauma, thus creating maladaptive behaviors and interpersonal challenges. In my opinion, any relationship with a white woman is an abusive relationship.

Has there ever been a time in your life when white folks have threatened you, either directly or indirectly, because of your race or skin color? Has there ever been a time in your life when they have called you derogatory, racist, or dehumanizing names because of your race or skin color? Have you ever been falsely accused of being intimidating or threatening? How about being accused of stealing, cheating, or not following "the rules"? Have you ever engaged in a conversation with a white person and experienced unnecessary emotional outbursts oozing with denial, minimization, and blame? And have you ever in your lifetime pointed out a white person's racism only to have them refute you, say they didn't mean it, and/or turn the tables on you and declare reverse racism?

I'm not sure how much you know about domestic violence relationships, but all the scenarios I mentioned in the previous paragraph are classic abuser tactics: strategic and deliberate actions used to abuse you while your abuser denies the abuse and/or works to make you think you're imagining it. And if you look closely at the Duluth Model's Power and Control Wheel, developed by the Domestic Abuse Intervention Programs (DAIP), you will see this cycle of violence clearly illustrated. Just like a domestic violence relationship, being in a relationship (or even just engaging) with a white person is agreeing to be emotionally and/or psychologically abused. How can it not be? White people collectively hold the "power" and they are members of the "privileged" group.

And no matter how awakened, liberal, and progressive white folks proclaim to be, their unearned pseudo-power and privilege is baked into their DNA. Their default setting is to think and operate from a place of power and privilege (aka White Authority), and power and privilege are the two main pillars and components of domestic violence abusers. There's bound to be violence. In fact, the violence is predictable and ongoing.

The condensed version of the cycle of violence goes like this: in the *Honeymoon Phase* (and you always meet covert racists in this phase), you meet a white person and think they are nice or cool. You chat, do lunch, talk at work, or maybe even hang out every now and then. Your new white acquaintance seems all right at first, but when the topics of racism and white terrorism come up, or they do something racist and you call them on it, things begin to change. A typical first response will be shock that you had the audacity to call them out, and then they will either deny or minimize their racism. They will say they didn't mean to offend you. They'll try to whitesplain what they really meant, and often they will become offended that you're offended.

CHAPTER THREE | WHITE WOMAN VIOLENCE 101

Just as expected, the Honeymoon Phase now transitions into the cycle of violence's *Tension-building Phase*. And if you're the slightest bit persistent in holding the white person accountable, they'll become emotionally brittle and either lash out right there on the spot or after they've stewed on the situation for a while. And the most "fragile" of white folks will say you're shaming and attacking them while naming you as the aggressor.

You are now actively in the cycle of violence's *Abuse Phase*. Your abuser's offense becomes nullified, and suddenly it is you who has the problem. The tables are turned. The next actions taken by white folks during this phase are exhausting and expected. When I have called white women out on their racism and violence, I have experienced both subtle and overt responses.

The more subtle acts of violence have been things like simply disappearing and going ghost (aka *White Silence*, a Weapon of Whiteness). Why is ghosting a form of violence? I'll use this example to illustrate it: imagine someone you barely know punches you in the gut, you confront them while you're lying on the ground, and they walk away, say nothing, and you never hear from them again. Poof! Like a ghost, they are gone, as if nothing ever happened. They have essentially denied their violence and added insult to injury by silently communicating that the violence did not occur and you're not worthy of or due their accountability. (And *denial* is one of the four D's of the intentions behind Weapons of Whiteness, as I discussed in Chapter 1.) Subtle acts of violence are abusive when used alone, and they are cumulatively and psychologically toxic and violent.

More overt acts of violence committed against me have been things like writing defaming blog posts, publishing negative articles about my work to shatter and stain my credibility, and calling my payment processing company to tell them I am a fraud and to file refund claims. Why? Because I pointed out words and behaviors that were racist and anti-black; in other words, I held white women accountable. That's it. That's all it takes for white women to become emotionally discombobulated and lash out with violence and vengeance. As I discussed in Chapter 2, this violence is why the phrase "white fragility" is an oxymoron. When issues of racism arise or are pointed out, white folks' emotional intolerance is not frail, it is manipulative, calculated, deliberate, and violent, just like the actions of an abuser. The sequence of behaviors is predictable and visible when you pay close attention.

The cycle of violence is called a "cycle" for a reason: because after the Abuse Phase, you will often find yourself back in the *Honeymoon Phase*. This time around, you may be feeling bruised, weary, and wary, but you receive intentional and profuse apologies, loving gestures, and empty promises of change. The abuser may express regret for their abusive attacks, do nice things, buy special gifts, and plead with you to give them another chance to prove their love, dedication, and/or commitment to you.

These moments serve to remind you there was once a "good" time in the relationship. And because you may have some affection or even love for the abuser, and/or because there may be children involved who love their parent, you are hopeful things really will change. You may believe what your abuser tells you, which creates another reason for you to stay in the relationship. And a trauma bond with the abuser makes leaving the situation or relationship even more difficult. (I will talk more about trauma bonding in Chapter 10.) The Honeymoon Phase can last for days, weeks, and even months, but it doesn't last forever.

You look back at your relationship and wonder why it took you so long to realize this person was an abuser. After all, they didn't suddenly start abusing. The deception and the dormant abusive tendencies have always been in them. Because they know no one is going to enter into a relationship with them with abuse happening straight out the gate, the Honeymoon Phase (especially the first time you go through it) is full of manipulative tactics to trick you into getting into the relationship and to set the trap of abuse.

And don't you for a second believe abusers don't know beforehand who they can lure into their treacherous traps. One myth you will hear about abusers is they are out of control. The exact opposite is true. They know precisely what they are doing and why they are doing it, and every behavior is calculated and deliberate. Think about it. If abusers were out of control, why aren't they abusing folks in the workplace? How come they don't show abusive behaviors when you first meet them? Because they know there are consequences for being violent on the job, and they know they can't show up abusive if they want to start a relationship. Abusers are clever and strategic.

I've worked in two domestic violence programs: one was a full-service program that included a safe house or shelter for women who had escaped domestic abuse; the other was a similar program, but it did not provide safe-house services. As a certified domestic violence and sexual assault advocate and trainer, I deeply understand the cycle of violence, which is why I am able to create this critical parallel between domestic abuse and racial violence. And based on the many domestic violence survivors I've had the opportunity to work with, the number one reason survivors stay in abusive relationships is fear. Fear of literally dying. Fear of losing their children. Fear of the police not believing them. Fear of the abuse getting worse if they attempt to leave. This fear is legitimate and justified, and only the survivor knows the potential for what can happen in their situation. This kind of fear never goes away, even when things are going "good" in the relationship or if the survivor is lucky enough to escape the violence.

Of course, there is more to this toxic and deadly cycle of violence, and you know that's true for sure if you've been in an abusive relationship. I encourage you to do your due diligence to better understand this cycle's deep psychological roots and tactics. It is important I make the parallel between the cycle of domestic violence and the violence white women inflict on Black people.

Prior to my own awakening, there were so many times when encounters with white women left me feeling irritated, violated, and confused. Now that I fully understand what white woman violence is, I am one hundred percent sure little white girls were weaponizing their whiteness against me as early as elementary school. And they definitely were in my middle and high school years. I felt their attacks, but I did not understand why they were trying to harm me. It wasn't until my forties that I began to psychologically dissect the toxic ways of white women. I was able to frame their toxicity in a way that made sense to me and that I could communicate to others.

CHAPTER THREE | WHITE WOMAN VIOLENCE 101

Now Beckyism (aka white woman violence) is crystal clear to me. And it is my duty and joy to share what I know to help you not let Becky or Brad psychologically kill you. Death by white woman violence is slow, methodical, and often inconspicuous. It is death by a thousand paper cuts. Yet if you are tuned into it, it's also very predictable, calculated, and universal. Unless a white woman is deeply dedicated to uprooting and eradicating her own racism, white terrorism, and anti-blackness, the toxic behaviors I have described in this chapter should be expected from her. And even those who are on the journey of becoming an effective and non-violent ally or accomplice will slip back into their default settings and cause psychological harm, because the tendency for violence is in their cells.

Remember the narcissistic behaviors I listed at the beginning of this chapter, behaviors like denial, trivializing, and false accusations? Add going silent, becoming emotionally brittle, whitesplaining, thinking they are exceptional, and vengeful retaliation, and you have an even better understanding of white women's default settings. It is rare to not experience these behaviors from white women (and white folks in general).

When engaging with white people about racism and white terrorism, you will inevitably experience at least one of the previously described behaviors. And when I say "engaging with," I mean having discussions about racism that include you pointing out their racist behaviors. Think about it. Does this ring true for you? It does for me. I have yet to meet and/or engage with a white woman and not experience these types of responses and behaviors. During my two-day intensive workshops for women I see different white faces in different cities, but the responses to discussing racism are the same: violent!

These responses are predictable and sometimes hilarious! Not because they are funny at all, but because I always know how white women will respond. And the reason I know, probably much like you, is due to what I call the *"White Woman Script."* White women recite this script with consistency, theatrics, and perfection. I am convinced white women are literally taught this script from the day they exit the womb. They are taught directly and indirectly by the white women who raise them: their mothers, grandmothers, sisters, and aunts.

As I mentioned in Chapter 1, I have noticed while doing my anti-racism work for the past five years that the phrases white women say during conversations about racism are damn near exact. In every single city I have visited to facilitate my workshops, the dialogue is fundamentally the same. And sometimes verbatim! There is yet to be a city where a white woman's comments and conversation about racism are unique. I've yet to be able to say, "Wow! This is different. I've never heard this before." As for this situation being hilarious, what I find funny is white women truly believe their responses are unique and original. They often get frustrated when I declare I already know what they are thinking and what they're about to say.

The White Woman Script is full of classic responses that you too may be familiar with. And to be clear, white men and other white folks use this script as well. But white women in particular have truly mastered this violent message, and it has become their muse. And it's their dangerous default. It often looks like this: first shock, then denial, defensiveness, brittleness, tears, and verbal lashing out. And although this is the classic order of responses, the script can begin with any of these reactions. If you ask a typical white woman if she is racist, the answer is likely to be no. (And when I say "typical," I mean white women who are not actively working toward being anti-racist and not intentionally trying to dismantle the system of white supremacy.) They will then say something you've heard from other white folks. Three common phrases you'll hear are, "I'm not racist, my partner/in-laws/friend is Black/Brown," "How can I be racist when I have Black/Brown/mixed-race children?" and "You don't know me; how can you call me racist?" Have you heard these phrases before? I could write a whole chapter on just the White Woman Script, but what I am trying to highlight is that these responses are predictable, and they are frequently used by white women when you confront their racism.

Where did they learn this script? Who taught them these phrases? Why do most white women use these same phrases within every industry in different cities across the country? I imagine white mothers don't use this generations-old, tattered script to teach their daughters the catchphrases of predatory behavior or narcissistic abuse tactics. I don't see them (well, most of them) sitting around the dining room table practicing the use of Weapons of Whiteness the same way they teach the alphabet. And I doubt white mothers and aunts encourage their daughters and nieces to pursue a Masters of Arts in interpersonal violence.

Yet white women have memorized all the violent phrases. They know the Weapons of Whiteness by heart.

They indeed have received a master's degree in interpersonal violence, and some have earned a doctorate degree with honors. The truth is the curriculum begins the instant the umbilical cord is cut. And the treacherous teachings begin with the core Weapon of Whiteness I call *White Superiority*.

White folks in the United States have always believed the false narratives of white supremacy and White Superiority, even those who live in marry-your-cousinville, who ain't got a pot to piss in or a window to throw it out of, and who can't put a literate sentence together to save their lives. The poorest of the poor and the most uneducated white folks still believe they are genetically superior to billionaire-status Black folks in spite of the overwhelming, well-documented, scientific proof that all humans, biologically speaking, have the same internal organs and bleed the same red blood.

And don't you be hoodwinked by those liberal, progressive, Black-Lives-Matter-shouting white folks either. Behind their deceptive facade is a white person who still believes they are superior to Black folks, whether it is a conscious belief or not. Because when has the world ever told them any differently? They all live in this delusion.

I'm sure you are already familiar with the many white women lurking in Black spaces, regurgitating what they've learned from Black folks, and still fully armed with Weapons of Whiteness. Some of them are so good you will catch yourself slipping! You'll believe they are doing the work because they have mastered the performance of being a fake ally who knows how to talk the talk in order to deflect attention from their innate violence. This deeply entrenched belief of White Superiority is at the crux of all other Weapons of Whiteness, and white women become indoctrinated into the pseudo-supremacy with their first out-of-the-womb breath. And those who have children go on to breed more abusers who will harm future generations of Black people. Racism hasn't ended, because white women keep having children who they then indoctrinate into white terrorism while claiming they are not part of the problem.

White women learn from the white women in their lives how to play the role of an entitled, privileged, and innocent victim that needs to be centered, coddled, and cared for at the expense of others' feelings, needs, and desires—especially Black women's. The white woman violence curriculum includes lessons on how to make everything about them, how to shamelessly be the center of attention, how to talk over and interrupt Black women, how to dismiss the pain and plight of Black folks (especially Black women), how to treat Black folks like they are invisible, how to reach over Black folks and walk into them in public spaces, how to believe the color blindness myth, how to cry at the slightest feeling of racial stress, and how to use Black bodies for pleasure and profit.

And these are the CliffsNotes. Trust and believe this curriculum of violence is a constant, consistent, and cumulative course on how to, as Rachael Edwards says, "Cut you in the dark and then ask you why you're bleeding." To make the bleeding more intense, white women will cry while they ask you why you're bleeding, and they'll pretend you are the one who harmed them. This violence is often intangible, invisible, and deeply insidious, which makes it hard to identify and name. And that just makes it easier for white women to deny they are committing violence, while weaponizing your uncertainty against you to make you feel "crazy" and/or overreactive. All this treachery and trauma is just violent narcissism 101.

Sounds like a classic episode of *The Twilight Zone*, doesn't it? Because it is. Luring and entrapping people into the twilight zone is a classic tactic of abusers, manipulators, and narcissists. This behavioral trait is their trademark. If you want to know whether someone is narcissistic or has narcissistic traits, look for whether they cause the twilight zone effect in you. You will be able to identify it by the person's uncanny way of causing harm to you emotionally and psychologically, whether implicitly or explicitly, and then acting surprised when you call the behavior out. They will then take the wounding deeper by refuting your truth that they've harmed you, or by telling you either that they didn't mean it or that you're imagining it. They will fight tooth and nail to refute their violence. And the ones who have mastered this manipulative behavior will cause you to second-guess yourself about the truth of your experiences, leaving you irritable and anxious. Then after being harmed, traumatized, and victimized to the point where you've had enough, you'll blow up on them or lash out, they'll sit back while you make a scene, and everyone around you will think you've lost your mind.

Case in point: when the white security guard or loss prevention staff follows you in the store and you know you are being followed. You're frustrated and angry. You know they are following you because you're Black, but you can't prove it. You have lost count of how many times this has happened to you. And on this occasion, you just can't take the profiling and dehumanization anymore, and you go off on the white person following you.

Guess what happens next? The security guard sees you as the aggressor, even though it's their behavior that is clearly premeditated and predatory. They are essentially stalking you. When you ask, "Why are you following me?" their first response will be denial. They will flat-out lie and say they were not following you when you damn well know they were. And if you show the slightest twinge of anger, it is highly likely the police will be called and/or you will suffer physical violence. This narcissistic act is perpetrated against Black people every single day, and sometimes several times in one day. This is just one example of the millions of paper cuts and worse that are perpetrated on Black bodies while in the presence of white bodies.

I will share a personal example of how white woman violence played out in my life. I was waiting in line at a grocery store. (This shit seems to happen to me quite often in stores!) When it was my turn to put my groceries on the counter, I noticed a middle-aged, visibly irritated white woman hovering over my back. Clearly, she was impatient for some reason, and my hunch was she was simply irked by my Black presence. So now I was feeling annoyed while minding my own Black-ass business. I put my groceries on the checkout counter, but before I could finish, she reached over my left arm to grab the thingamajig you use to separate grocery orders, and she slammed it down on the counter. There wasn't even two inches of space available for her to put her groceries on the belt. She did not care. She started stacking her things one by one with the same "hurry up and get out of my way" attitude that Walmart Wendy from Chapter 1 displayed.

I took a deep breath, ignored her, and moved toward the cashier. While the cashier was ringing up my items, the white woman came right up on my side with an item and asked the cashier if she could price-check it. The cashier, who was Latina, ignored her. I looked all upside the white broad's face, and by this time, I was pissed. She again asked the cashier to price-check the item. In fact, she insisted, while dangling the item in the cashier's face.

That was it. I was done. I turned to the white woman and said, "Can you wait until I'm finished checking out before you barge in and get all up on me!" She was instantly startled and shocked I was confronting her violence. Unlike other white women I've had similar encounters with, she shut the hell up and didn't say another word. Her face turned red, and she looked extremely ashamed and embarrassed to the point of putting her head down (as she should). The cashier looked at me, smiled, and continued to ring up my items. I gathered my bags, put them in the shopping cart, and left the store.

On my way out, I looked back at the white woman, and she had returned to her demanding behavior. Whew, child! I was livid. I was so mad I had to talk myself down while walking to my car. Thank God it was a cold day because I surely needed to cool the f*ck down! I'm not exactly sure why this tends to happen in grocery stores with white women, but let me just say this was not the first time, nor will it be the last, that a white woman doesn't see, hear, or respect me while I'm bothering no one and just existing in my beautiful Black skin.

So, let's replay this scenario. I am minding my own business and causing harm to no one. Then a random, entitled white woman invades my physical space and demands to be served and attended to while the cashier is serving me. And when the white woman notices she is not the center of attention and being catered to, she becomes aggressive and demanding. When she is called out for her invasive and violent behavior, she is shocked and can't believe I would fix my mouth to speak to her in that way, a way that to her mind is "not a Black woman's place." Her not verbally responding to me holding her accountable is rare; most times, white women get tearful, verbally assaultive, and show their asses to me. But in this case, this woman's sense of guilt or perhaps fear (because you know anytime a Black woman stands up for herself white women get afraid) caused her to shut the hell up! Had she not, who knows what would have happened, because I am tired of white woman violence and would not have been silent. I refuse to be silent. This type of shit is draining. And every time we encounter this unyielding violence, it extracts emotional life from us. We expend precious energy, life source, and labor just defending our right to exist. White woman violence is real, rampant, and ravishes the lives of Black folks with a relentless thirst for Black pain and Black labor.

I often compare white women and their violence to zombies, like those hideous and blood-thirsty creatures in the movie *Night of the Living Dead*. And while this comparison may sound harsh, if you really think about it, it's not far-fetched. The ghouls in that movie had two distinct characteristics or behaviors: they were dead inside because of a toxic radiation infection, and they relentlessly hunted for living human flesh.

I have discovered over the past five years that white women have the same two characteristics. First, they are apathetic about the pain and plight of Black folks; in other words, they are dead inside. Second, white women have always systematically hunted Black bodies in a variety of forms for their personal pleasure and profit. And the truth is, there has never been a time in this country when white women (and white people) have not exhibited these zombie-like characteristics and behaviors.

LAY DOWN YOUR WEAPONS

WHITE ENTITLEMENT: When white folks believe they are entitled to consume time, space, and conversations in order to be the center of attention, and when they expect to be taught, considered, and forgiven.

How are you wielding the weapon of entitlement to take up space from more marginalized Black people?

_____

_____

_____

_____

WHITE AUTHORITY: When white folks use their whiteness to dominate Black and Brown folks: speaking for and over, interrupting, taking up space, cutting in line, and dismissing their presence. Also, when white people think they are better than and/or know what is best for nonwhite people.

How are you showing up as the "authority" on blackness and potentially causing harm to Black people?

_____

_____

_____

_____

WHITE PADDY ROLLING: When white folks act like slave patrols by policing Black bodies and reporting them to the "authorities" and/or making "citizen's arrests."

How are you paddy rolling other Black people? How are you policing their choices and actions?

_____

_____

_____

_____

WHITE DOG WHISTLING: When white folks use dangerous and coded language to passively incite violence against Black and Brown folks and/or to summon the lynch mob.

What coded language do you use to sound the dog whistle on other Black people?

_____

_____

_____

_____

> IT IS CERTAIN, IN ANY CASE, THAT IGNORANCE, ALLIED WITH POWER, IS THE MOST FEROCIOUS ENEMY JUSTICE CAN HAVE.

JAMES BALDWIN

CHAPTER FOUR

WHITE TERRORISM

> There's never been a time when white folks
> have not terrorized black folks.
>
> Catrice M. Jackson

Can you name a specific time in American history, up to and including now, when white people by the hundreds of thousands took to the streets to demand the freedom, liberation, and justice of Black people? I'm not talking about the "good" white folks who marched with Martin Luther King Jr. back in the day. Nor am I talking about the white folks who show up at a Black Lives Matter march. I am talking about participation levels like those at the Million Man March in 1995 or the Women's March in 2017. I'm talking about a time when white folks shut down highways, stormed government buildings, boycotted businesses, went on strike, or disrupted societal norms in the name of freedom, liberation, and justice for Black lives. A time when white folks, the collective white folks, put their lives, money, and resources on the line to say, "No more violence against Black bodies." Can you name a time since 1619?

And can you count the number of days in this country when there has not been an attack on Black lives? I can. The number is zero! Not one single damn day! From 1619 to this moment as you are reading this book, Black folks have been continuously hunted, abused, dehumanized, and used for pleasure and profit by white folks. We have been mistreated, marginalized, murdered, and oppressed in every way possible, nonstop, every single day since we arrived here. And not just by white folks, but by everyone, including non-Black people of color (NBPOC) and Indigenous peoples. And sadly, I must include Black folks as perpetrators of violence against Black folks. Damn! Oh yes, I will cover this type of violence in later chapters.

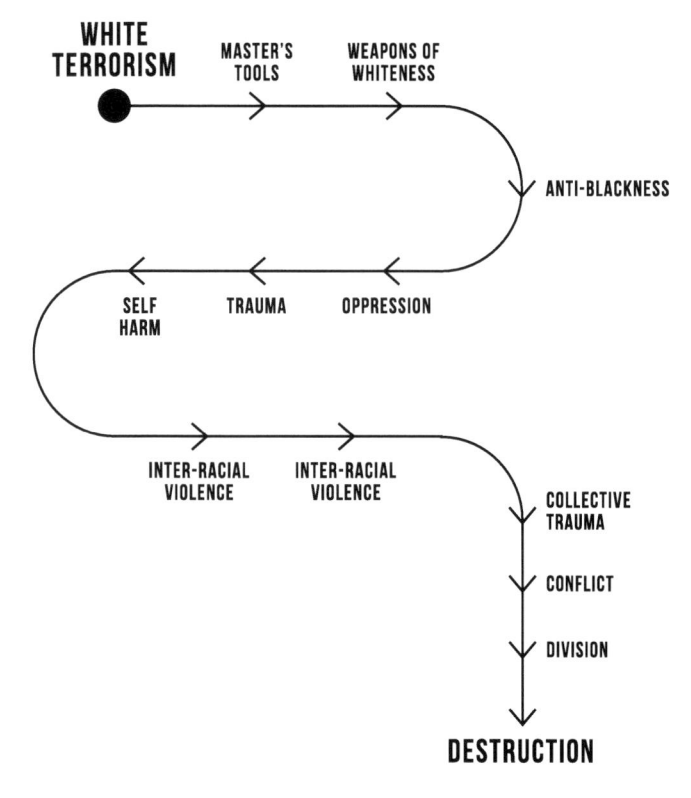

```
WHITE TERRORISM → MASTER'S TOOLS → WEAPONS OF WHITENESS → ANTI-BLACKNESS → OPPRESSION → TRAUMA → SELF HARM → INTER-RACIAL VIOLENCE → INTER-RACIAL VIOLENCE → COLLECTIVE TRAUMA → CONFLICT → DIVISION → DESTRUCTION
```

There is only one word to accurately describe this white thirst for Black bodies, Black blood, and Black lives: terrorism. According to dictionary.com, terrorism is defined as "the use of threats and violence to intimidate and coerce, especially for political purposes." Synonyms for terrorism include homicide, lynching, massacre, bloodshed, shooting, assassination, manslaughter, oppression, and cruelty. When you think about what has happened, and continues to happen, to Black folks in America, you can see we have experienced every one of those acts systemically, systematically, and intentionally from white people since day one. The unfathomable terrorism Black folks have endured in this country is not by chance or coincidence; it is by diabolical and deliberate design. The FBI and Homeland Security recently released statistics showing that in the past eighteen years, white males have committed more acts of violence/terrorism in the United States than any other group of people.

Duh! Really? Only in the last eighteen years! Bullshit. Didn't chattel slavery last almost three hundred years? White amnesia is one helluva drug, isn't it? I mean, it's got white folks forgetting and denying their history of violence, beginning with the damn-near annihilation of the Indigenous peoples of North America; all the horrendous acts of viciousness to the Black and Brown folks residing on this continent; and the founding fathers' fundamental acts of violence, including slavery. Apparently white America has also conveniently forgotten about not only the Rosewood massacre, but also the Black Wall Street massacre that preceded it, where the United States government dropped bombs on American soil to wipe out innocent Black Americans who had the audacity to thrive within their own community. That was the epitome of domestic terrorism, but somehow this purposeful atrocity doesn't count as terrorism.

And this violence is unrelenting today, with the terrorism Black folks face at the hands of racist policies like stop-and-frisk, mass incarceration, and police brutality. I could write an entire series of books about the white violence committed against Black folks and still never capture it all. Yet even though you may not need to be persuaded, I believe it's important to make the case for why and how white folks have never stopped terrorizing Black folks in America, and how white treachery has infected us too.

I wrote this book for you, Black people, so I will not dredge up too many explicit atrocities perpetrated against Black bodies. I know it can be triggering and traumatizing to keep hearing these wretched stories. I don't like to hear these truths repeatedly either, but they do serve as a reminder of what our ancestors suffered and what many of us are still enduring today. However, I will reference a few cases to make a point and/or to offer some potentially new knowledge to Black folks who may not know the extensive list of transgressions committed by white people against us.

This violence stems from two major goals: first, to maintain a deeply flawed sense of white supremacy; and second, to serve the cause of social and racial control, which allows white people to inflict and sustain systematic oppression. An example of this is lynching, which was one of the most inhumane acts of violence perpetrated against Black bodies in the United States. Historians debate when lynching began and ended (and whether it really has ended), but in a 2018 *Guardian* article titled, "How white Americans used lynchings to terrorize and control black people," Lartey and Morris stated, "[Lynchings] became widely practiced in the US south from roughly 1877, the end of post-civil war reconstruction, through 1950." Hmmm... the first enslaved Africans arrived in America in 1619, and I highly doubt it took two hundred plus years (to 1877) for lynching to commence. Y'all already know these historians and history books are white-washed lies, but anyway!

We know Black folks were accused of crimes they did not commit. We know organized and unauthorized lynch mobs hunted them down. We know they were beaten, hung, and set on fire for the real crime of being Black. Here's a fact you may not know: white folks would often dismember Black folks' bodies and take body parts for souvenirs. But not before they put on their Sunday best and dolled up their kids to take them to watch lynchings, those sinister shows of apathy and animalistic behavior.

Lynching Black folks was a sport, a white tradition, and an evil entertainment for these people who claim to be supreme beings. "Sadistic" is what you call this type of behavior and engagement. No other word accurately describes these horrific acts of violence. Can you imagine taking your children, grandchildren, or nieces and nephews to watch someone be hanged, set on fire, and dismembered? What is going on in the minds of people who do this? There is something fundamentally and innately wrong with these sorts of folks. A word from the field of psychology that describes them is "antisocial."

Two classic traits of antisocial people are they cause harm to others and they have a negative effect on society. (The phrases "a defect in moral character" and "mental insanity" were used to describe those with antisocial behaviors in the early 1800s.) Antisocial people are also impulsive, reckless, aggressive, and lack the ability to show empathy or remorse for those they hurt. I am essentially describing traits of antisocial personality disorder (ASPD). And a person doesn't usually obtain an ASPD diagnosis unless there is evidence of genetic inheritance. Yes, that means parents pass down these aggressive and apathetic genes to their children.

In addition, ASPD is exacerbated by environmental factors, such as learned behaviors modeled by parents, caregivers, and society. Plainly stated, the genes and learned behaviors for this violence and aggression were highly likely to have been passed down for at least four hundred years. According to the American Psychological Association (APA), personality disorders are difficult to diagnose, and personality disorder theories focus primarily on inborn or inherited traits.

I certainly do not want to give white folks any excuses for their violence and/or violent tendencies. On the other hand, as a mental health professional, I can't help but see the correlation and overlap between the centuries of white violence and how the APA defines antisocial behavior. When I think about the four centuries of brutality and violence committed by white folks against Black bodies (and the white bystanders who did very little to stop it), genetic inheritance and learned behavior go hand-in-hand as a sound rationale for why these violent behaviors were repeated by white folks with few or no consequences.

What's interesting is white folks today like to say they are nothing like their ancestors. They say slavery is over, that Black folks should get over it and just let it go, and "I didn't own any slaves!" But what the collective white folks fail to talk about is genetic inheritance. It's as if they believe the genes of violence, aggression, and apathy magically disappeared from the descendants of "those" white folks of the past. Well, I do not think those genes have gone anywhere, because white violence is still happening. It just doesn't look like enslavement or like the barbaric act of lynching a Black body with a rope. These days, white violence is far more insidious.

To be silent, uninterested in, and/or apathetic about what continues to happen to Black people in America is a form of violence. It is what I would call "bystander violence." And while there were some white folks who spoke up in the past and those who speak up now, there have not been enough white folks taking action to stop the violence. Collectively, white folks are still dressing up in their Sunday best and sitting by as Black bodies are attacked and destroyed. Many of them directly and indirectly contribute to the violence by not committing to being anti-racist, which entails creating and embodying an anti-racism plan. Collective white apathy about the Black experience is palpable and pandemic. White folks have inherited this apathy even if they don't know it, but lack of awareness doesn't make their apathy any less sinister.

Where did this genetic inheritance of violence come from? Has there ever been a time when white bodies have not been violent against Black bodies, and other bodies too, for that matter? How did white folks get this way? I have been pondering and searching for answers for the past five years, and I have developed a few insights.

Resmaa Menakem, MSW, LICSW, author of *My Grandmother's Hands: Racialized Trauma and the Pathway to Mending Our Hearts and Bodies*, talks about white-body supremacy and states, "...white bodies traumatized each other in Europe for centuries before they encountered black and red bodies. This carnage and trauma profoundly affected white bodies and the expressions of their DNA." He goes on to say, "...the historical trauma of white bodies is closely linked to the development of white-body supremacy in America." Menakem points out that violence was rampant in England as far back as the 1500s. People were burned at the stake, and torture chambers existed in which human bodies were stretched and pulled apart with a device known as the rack. The medieval period (aka the Middle Ages) was primitive, barbaric, and grotesque. There is a brutal history of violence in Europe.

The participation in and the witnessing of these horrendous acts not only registered in the minds of Europeans, they also were most certainly passed down from one generation to the next. This treachery and violence are among the reasons Europeans left their violent land to come to America, but they brought the violence and dis-ease with them, stored in their DNA. Menakem does an excellent job of describing white folks' historical violence. I refer to it as "calling a thing a thing," and this thing is "white-on-white crime." If you haven't read Menakem's book, get it now and dive in.

This white-on-white violence is trauma, and as Menakem says, "...trauma lives in bodies." And I know this for sure: if you do not heal yourself from trauma, you will pass it on to your children. Trauma is contagious and genetically transferred. White folks have been passing trauma on to their children for over five centuries. Can you imagine the bloodshed and horror that occurred among white folks during this period?

Violent thoughts, behaviors, energies, and responses are, simply put, part of white (European) culture, whether they own up to this unvarnished truth or not. And I'm a firm believer that if research indicates the trauma of chattel slavery was passed on to the descendants of enslaved Africans, there is no way in hell that violence was *not* passed on to the offspring of white folks. I don't need to reference a scientific study to know that's true. All you have to do is to look at the history and track record of white folks in this country. There is a consistent, persistent, and pervasive trail of blood, violence, and trauma linked to the first Europeans who set foot in America, and to every generation thereafter. And the trauma inflicted by white folks onto Black folks is in turn stored in our bodies.

Dr. Joy DeGruy, author of *Post Traumatic Slave Syndrome: America's Legacy of Enduring Injury and Healing*, talks about the behaviors, actions, and beliefs of African Americans and the multi-generational trauma they experience as a result of racist violence. For twelve years, she compiled quantitative and qualitative data on the residual impact of chattel slavery on the descendants of the Trans-Atlantic Slave Trade's victims. I am so grateful for DeGruy's work and the foundation she laid for us to truly understand the devastating effects of centuries of brutality against Black bodies.

When I was growing up, I knew nothing about post-traumatic slave syndrome (PTSS), and my mother did not teach us about the emotional, spiritual, physiological, and psychological aftermaths of this atrocity. What I find both frustrating and interesting is that in my family, no one talked about what slavery did to its descendants. It was like a family secret everyone knew about but never discussed. The only time I remember talking to my mother about slavery was when the original Roots mini-series aired in 1977, and we watched the whole show together. My mom would tell stories about what it was like growing up in the Jim Crow era, but not much about slavery and its adverse effects on Black people post-slavery. I wonder why. Fortunately, my mother is still living, so I can get answers to that question.

How about you? Did you discuss how PTSS was affecting Black people in your community when you were growing up? My theory about why my mother didn't talk about PTSS is because she was so busy trying to survive in a white system that wanted her to fail, she didn't have the time and energy to worry about the past. My mother was single, Black, and disabled, which means she had plenty of challenges and barriers to surmount. She was trying to make ends meet, she was busy scratching and surviving, and that's what she gave her attention to and talked about the most. I think many Black folks back in the day were just glad to be "free" (not physically enslaved) and trying to survive. And this mentality is a byproduct of PTSS. A mindset of fear, struggle, and some variation of hopelessness. My mother never talked explicitly about her race-related fears, but I felt them often in her efforts to scratch and survive. And on occasion, she would break down, because the scuffle of life was too hard, and she felt like every time she took one step forward, the system forced her to take two steps back. Trying to survive on a fixed income while raising two children was a financial struggle for my mother, but she always made a way out of no way.

Her story is not all that unique. My story is not all that unique. Our stories of fear, struggle, and variations of hopelessness are commonplace for a lot of Black folks in America, primarily because the unceasing white terrorism has systematically dismembered families. Centuries of chattel slavery sexually exploited and sexually terrorized Black women, while Black men were sold away from their families and emasculated. Black families were torn apart, and once they were finally free from enslavement, many Black folks were not able to psychologically escape the indoctrination of servitude, white supremacy, and anti-blackness. They were free from their chains, but they were mentally conditioned to bondage, because they carried that historical trauma in their DNA.

When you intermingle white folks who have post-traumatic stress disorder (PTSD) with Black folks who have post-traumatic slave syndrome (PTSS), you create a perfect and ferocious storm. White folks were able to quickly and easily wield their unhealed trauma as a lethal weapon against nonwhite folks. And they did so with precision and deliberate intention.

White terrorism. That's what it was, and what it still is today. This terrorism is not depicted or inflicted like it was during the medieval period or during chattel slavery. It has morphed into biased laws, slave patrol practices, and legal-yet-fatal personal interactions. White terrorism today looks like stop-and-frisk laws or calling the police on Black people for taking pictures in a park with their children or for taking a nap in their dorm room (loitering laws). It looks like corrupt criminal justice and judicial systems that result in mass incarceration of Black folks. It looks like an illegal and unethical chokehold that causes Black men to say, "I can't breathe," and die. It looks like a suspicious death (declared a suicide) of an outspoken and kind Black woman in a Texas jail. It looks like Black women dying in childbirth because the healthcare system believes Black women have no value and are dispensable. White terrorism looks like a Black boy not being able to play with a toy gun in a park. It looks like a young mother being stalked in her own home and being shot while sitting next to her five-year-old son. And it looks like nine Black people being shot in church by a racist mass murderer.

Inhumane enslavement, buck breaking, wench breeding, forced wet nursing, serial raping, pedophilia, lynching, and mass murders. Lynch mobs, cross burnings, church bombings, massacres, assassinations, stealing and selling organs from Black bodies, and white people enslaving their own mixed-race children.

All these violent behaviors and more are central to the ever-evolving and endless legacy of white America. And while most white folks did not explicitly participate in these barbaric and gruesome actions, they didn't actively participate in stopping them either. White Silence is complicit in this violence, and the collective denial of our truth is the most violent form of gaslighting by white folks.

When I think about the many ways people can terrorize each other, white folks have done it all. They have left no stone unturned and have not refused one single opportunity to commit violence against Black bodies. They have never said, "Nah, we'll sit this one out." They have never refused to act inhumanely toward Black people. Never. Can you name a time when they have refused such an opportunity since 1619?

And this persistent, incessant, and pervasive violence is not just *explicitly* wielded against us. White people also wield *implicit* biases, pseudo- (aka fake-ass) supremacy, and nefarious anti-blackness against us as naturally as breathing. Implicit acts of violence are evident in their stares and glares (the White Gaze), and the clutching of their purses and pearls. These acts are evident in falsifying reports and testimonies. They are evident in hiring practices and dismissive customer service. They are evident in moving as far away as possible from Black folks and following Black folks in stores. Both explicit and implicit white violence and white terrorism are evident in over-patrolling Black neighborhoods, refusing to provide Black patients with adequate pain medicine, and calling the cops on Black people for no damn reason. This terrorism is evident in white folks reaching over you, cutting in line, calling the manager, and walking into you as if you're invisible. It's also evident in using the colorblind lie to manipulate you, the fetishizing of Black bodies, and loving Black culture while hating Black people.

White terrorism is so common it shows up daily in simple conversations with white folks. White terrorism is so intrinsic for white folks you don't even have to engage with them personally for violence to occur, because white terrorism has been written into policies and procedures, the laws, the constitution, and essentially everything white folks create.

Sadly, there is no safe place or space where you can be shielded from white violence and terrorism. When you wake up in the morning, you can see it in the news in the form of racially biased journalism, cultural appropriation, and racially charged dog whistles. While driving to work, you can see it happening in the streets disguised as a "typical" traffic stop. Once you arrive at work, it is certain Becky or Brad will unleash Weapons of Whiteness against you. You can be sure the white customers or clients you serve will terrorize you with stares, glares, and gaslighting. While you're at work, your children are being violated and traumatized at school, predominantly by emotionally abusive Beckys and Karens. You can see the same shit on your drive home, while hoping and praying you do not get stopped by the police. When you get home from work, you can see more white violence on the television, and you know the terror can knock at your door or kick it in to violate or murder you. I don't care what white folks say, all this is very real, very true, and very detrimental to the lives of Black people. All Black people.

It is important to repeat that white violence is contagious, inherited, and learned, and white terrorism is transferrable. Unfortunately, Black folks have also been infected by toxic whiteness, and its terroristic traits have been unknowingly transmitted into our bodies and minds. We may not have realized this transference was happening. But white folks, the original hosts of this infectious dis-ease, have been willfully passing it on to us and teaching us how to pass it on to other Black folks and NBPOC. And they've been doing so for as long as they've been on this continent. I'm talking about the strategic transmission of anti-blackness. Violence from the same source of white terrorism, but a different shade.

This sinister strategy of anti-blackness is so ubiquitous that it's just as deadly as more overt forms of white terrorism, even if it's often invisible and unconscious. So invisible and unconscious that we then pass it on by infecting our offspring with this lethal infection of self-loathing and self-sabotage. We have been so skillfully indoctrinated into anti-blackness, and conditioned to hate ourselves so exceptionally well, we are now using the master's tools to control, manipulate, and harm one another. Sadly, even when we have cut our strings, we still often dance to the puppet master's tune. We have become the master's tools.

LAY DOWN YOUR WEAPONS

WHITE ANTAGONISM: When white folks agitate, irritate, and purposely trigger Black and Brown folks with racial comments and behaviors.

What statements or behaviors do you use against other Black people that you know will trigger and antagonize them?

___

___

___

___

WHITE CODES: When white folks use a set of conscious and unconscious rules, guidelines, standards, and expectations to try to control and deny the agency and sovereignty of Black folks.

What rules, guidelines, or "Black Codes" do you use to exclude other Black folks, and/or to control their agency?

___

___

___

___

WHITE GASLIGHTING: When white folks use silence, denial, and/or minimization to emotionally agitate Black and Brown folks before and after racial assaults.

How do you gaslight Black folks when they call you out on your anti-blackness or colorism?

_____

_____

_____

_____

WHITE APATHY: When white folks don't give a damn about Black and Brown folks and fail to ensure nonwhite lives are safe and protected.

In what ways are you not giving a damn about Black folks or "certain kinds" of Black folks?

_____

_____

_____

_____

THE MASTER'S TOOLS WILL NEVER DISMANTLE THE MASTER'S HOUSE. THEY MAY ALLOW US TEMPORARILY TO BEAT HIM AT HIS OWN GAME, BUT THEY WILL NEVER ENABLE US TO BRING ABOUT GENUINE CHANGE.

AUDRE LORDE
SISTER OUTSIDER: ESSAYS AND SPEECHES

CHAPTER FIVE

THE MASTER'S TOOLS

Toxic whiteness is so virulent it will still harm Black people even if the hosts were to suddenly be eliminated.

Catrice M. Jackson

"For the master's tools will never dismantle the master's house." Audre Lorde, a writer, feminist, womanist, and civil rights activist, first uttered this accurate and profound sentence in 1979 during her speech at the New York Institute for the Humanities Conference. This infamous quote continues to reverberate throughout the world today, especially in social justice spaces. In short, Audre's quote is a multidimensional analysis and critique of the white supremacy that infiltrates and consumes the core of white feminism. She is alluding to how feminism, especially during her lifetime, has never centered and prioritized the lives of Black women. Ever.

The next sentence of Audre's speech states, *"They [the master's tools] may allow us temporarily to beat him at his own game, but they will never allow us to bring about genuine change."* Audre is clearly stating that with their version of feminism, white women have always put their feelings, desires, challenges, and needs before any other women's. She is also stating that equality, equity, liberation, and freedom will not

CHAPTER FIVE | THE MASTER'S TOOLS

come for any women if white women continue to use the tools of patriarchy against Black, Brown, and LGBTQ+ women.

Unfortunately, I did not discover this gem of a quote and absolute truth until about five years ago, but I am so grateful I did. Audre's words deeply resonate with me, and I believe they can lend great insight into the anti-blackness we inflict on one another. In this chapter, I'm going to offer my own interpretation of how "the master's tools" have served to harm everyone, but specifically Black people. And I will offer insights into why everyone uses these tools against Black people, including other Black people. The views I express in this chapter are my own and are not the words of master teacher Audre Lorde. Please reference her work to understand what she meant by her quote. However, I believe "the master's tools" quote is the perfect framework for analyzing, critiquing, and explaining just how slick and pervasive white terrorism (aka white supremacy) is. My hope is by reading this book you will learn how to begin dismantling the master's house and how to stop the violence we inflict on each other.

It is important for me to begin with a disclaimer, because I hope we are all on a journey to decolonize our minds, eradicate our internalized oppression, heal our own self-hatred, and take back our ancestral sovereignty. As a cis, heterosexual, lighter-skinned, formally educated, middle-class, able-bodied Black woman, I am aware not only of the many privileges I have, but also how I have consciously and unconsciously wielded them as weapons of human destruction. I am learning every day how I too am problematic as a result of these privileges, and I am working on being less harmful, especially to other Black folks. And I admit I am still struggling my way through and failing forward on this lifetime journey. It's so easy to be self-centered and in denial about the ways in which I cause harm to my fellow Black folks. Causing harm is not my natural way of being, but I am sure I have made (and will continue to make) mistakes as I strive to be a better human being. With that said, I am open for feedback, accepting of responsibility, and willing to be accountable for my missteps, harm, and evolution. This is truly the only way we can become better human beings and be less oppressive toward one another.

Several years ago, I made a comment on a Facebook post stating that when Black folks "teach" white folks how to be anti-racist, it is a gift to white people. I still believe this. But a Black queer woman (who I didn't know was queer) called me out in front of thousands of white folks and essentially said I was being arrogant and gaslighting them. First, I was floored! Totally taken aback, because I hadn't had any previous problems or issues with this woman. Second, it shocked me that she was caping for white folks (I still believe she was). I didn't understand why she was going so hard for them, especially over the comment I made, which I didn't think was arrogant or gaslighting.

Eventually, we took the conversation to a private space on Messenger. Long story short, she called me homophobic. It felt like a gut punch. No, better yet, a sucker punch, because I wasn't expecting it. My comment had absolutely no homophobic tones, and I had no idea she was a queer woman. And while I will stand on my belief that the *comment* was not homophobic, she was right that *I* am. I didn't want to admit it then, but as I continue to do my own personal "be a better human" work, I've had to look in my dark places—those places we all have that we'd prefer not to examine.

It is uncomfortable to look at and accept all the ways in which the privileges we have deny other folks their rights and liberties. Today I can say, "Yes, I am homophobic." And not because I am proud of it, but how can I not be? How can I not be when heteronormative is the default? How can I not be when society prioritizes and celebrates being straight and demonizes being lesbian, gay, or queer? How can I not be when we are taught at an early age that a person is either male or female? How can I not be when the media has programmed us to believe the only acceptable form of sexual attraction is heterosexual?

I have been indoctrinated into all that, and perhaps you have been too. As a result of this indoctrination, I have conscious and unconscious beliefs and actions that oppress, harm, and marginalize anyone who is different from society's *norms*. Sometimes I can catch these unconscious thoughts and beliefs and silence or correct them, and other times not so much. But I am committed to unlearning any and all ways of thinking and acting that cause harm to folks, especially to my Black folks.

The one thing I know for sure is defaults and norms cause a tremendous amount of violence and harm, specifically in the Black community, and these are just some of the "privileges" we wield against each other to cause trauma. These are just a few of the master's tools we continue to use, and they will not dismantle the master's house. Regarding the callout by this Black queer woman, it was the first time I was willing to look in the mirror she held up for me. And it does not matter whether

I think her holding it up was justified; I am glad she did. Even though I fully understand what it feels like to live within the society's margins as a fat Black woman, it doesn't give me the right to use the "privileges" I have against other Black folks, and it doesn't give you the right to do it either. Maybe you're thinking, "Catrice, I don't have any privileges!" Yes, you do. We all do in some form or fashion. It is a complete waste of time to argue you don't have any. Instead, focus on understanding which privileges you do have, own up to them, and then start doing your "be a better human being work" right now.

Before taking a deeper dive into the master's tools, I want to provide some perspective on what I mean by the word "privileges." There are many schools of thought on what I would call "unearned hierarchical advantages" or privileges. The most obvious advantages are the visible and/or prominent ones, such as ethnicity, skin complexion (tone/color), body size, gender, physical features, hair texture, physical disabilities (challenges), age (perceived or real), and language.

It is important to note these attributes are often measured against white norms; in other words, what white people deem acceptable. Meaning we Black folks measure ourselves or each other according to these white standards, which is one of the master's tools dating back to plantation life when Black people were pitted against one another. We have been consciously and unconsciously using white people's malicious measurements against each other for centuries. Other hierarchical advantages include things like class, religion, socioeconomic or social status, education, geographic location, occupation, sexual identity, and material possessions.

CHAPTER FIVE | THE MASTER'S TOOLS

I am realizing just how thoroughly Black people in America have been bamboozled, brainwashed, and psychologically altered by the *master*. And I must admit, my ongoing enlightenment makes me feel both sad and liberated. The systemic and systematic indoctrination has plagued us with a menacing, tragic, four-hundred-year-long graduate-level class in mind control, self-hatred, and anti-blackness. The more I learn about our people's plight and pain, the sadder I become, and I sometimes sink into moments of despair. Because, my God, how could one group of people do such horrendous things to another group of people? I cannot begin to fathom the horror and trauma Black folks experienced generations before me, and yet I am grateful for my ancestors' remarkable resiliency.

As for feeling liberated, with each new piece of historical information I uncover about the Black experience, I am also psychologically set free and my spirit of liberation expands and intensifies. Through it all I am clearer about just how much we have been taught to hate and harm each other because of so-called white "supremacy." One way or another, we are chasing the approval of something that doesn't exist and isn't even possible. There is no such thing as a superior person or a superior race. This fool's gold we chase has no value.

Think about it. Stop for a moment and reflect on what whiteness has done to Black bodies and minds all over the world. Think about how whiteness has methodically massacred and murdered thousands of Black and Brown bodies for no other reason than their skin colors. As I discussed in Chapter 2, whiteness has stolen land, raped and tortured women, kidnapped Black and Brown children, forced nonwhite children into boarding schools without their parents, forced Indigenous peoples off their lands, enslaved millions, built violent concentration camps, restructured plantations into prisons, and locked Brown children in cages. What the f*ck is supreme about that barbarism? Nothing. You hear me? Not a damn thing! Yet we have been brainwashed to believe there is something special and superior about whiteness.

Fool's gold, I'm telling you! There is nothing extraordinary about white brains, white thoughts, or white bodies. Go find me some legitimate fact-checked research data clearly illustrating this so-called superiority and I will consider it. These are lies, so why do so many of us still believe them to be true? 'Cause that's what mama nem told you? Nah! We need to listen to what Brother Malcom says. Because he is right! Who taught you to hate yourself? Who taught you to hate your Black brothers and sisters?

I too was brainwashed, but I am waking up from those sick lies every day. The violent veil has been lifted, and now I cannot help but see the fool's gold and lies for what they are. I pray that all the lies hiding in my subconscious be revealed to me. Then I can know the truth and reconcile my ignorance in my effort to be a better human being. And although I would love to say my hierarchical advantages or privileges are myths too, they hold unearned power I can use to help or harm my fellow Black folks who do not have the same privileges. My lighter skin affords me the opportunity to be perceived as more respectable, palatable, and "safe." And not only by white folks, but also by NBPOC and Black folks. There is a false assumption that because of my skin color, I am in closer proximity to whiteness, and therefore I am somehow better.

Let me be clearer. I am not superior because of my proximity to whiteness, but people assume I am. My advanced education affords me the opportunity to apply for and obtain jobs that those who do not have a formal education cannot apply for. Because I have a master's degree, the assumption is I am smarter than Black folks who do not. And although my education offers me insight that others may not have, it does not make me inherently wiser. My skin color and education are just two of the "privileges" I can use as weapons against other Black people; they are the master's tools. And I have used them consciously and unconsciously to cause harm.

THE MASTER'S TOOLS
How We Use Them to Harm Each Other

COLORISM

RESPECTIBILITY

CLASSISM

PROXIMITY TO WHITENESS

SHIFTING

ELITISM

WEAPONS OF WHITENESS

What hierarchical advantages or privileges do you have? Did you grow up in a two-parent household? Did you grow up in the city or the suburbs? Was your high school predominantly white, mostly Black, or diverse? Would you classify your skin tone or color as light, Black, or Brown? Something else? Did your family survive off public assistance, or did your parents or caregivers make good money? Are other ethnicities running through your veins? Do you consider yourself to be fat, skinny, obese, or fit? Would you say you are pretty, gorgeous, average, or ugly? Do you have advanced degrees, or did you drop out of high school?

The answers to these questions can lead you to understanding some of the privileges you do and don't have. And although this is just a short list of potential privileges, having even one of these means you can use it to cause harm. How are you using your privileges to harm other Black people? Is it through judgment, exclusion, or isolation? Weaponizing your privileges can also show up in avoidance, critique, denial, and dismissal.

Let's talk about judgment, exclusion, and isolation, and the not-so-obvious ways we weaponize our privileges and use the master's tools, which are rooted in anti-blackness and white terrorism. We judge each other by the texture of our hair. We judge each other by the way we speak. We judge each other's body size. We judge each other based on skin color. Nappy headed. Bad hair. Good hair. Ghetto. Ratchet. Ebonics. Light-bright. Midnight. I do not know any other "race" of people that uses food descriptors to describe their skin color. Chocolate. Caramel. Butterscotch. Why? What is the purpose? Is it just our way of adding flavor to everything we do? Or is it another way for us to separate ourselves into categories as a form of exclusion and othering? I recall several Black folks calling me bourgeois (bougie) at one time or another in my life. In my twenties and early thirties, I would have thought this description was a noble one. A time when I was drinking the master's Kool-Aid and drunk on it. Today I really do not care for the word and how it is used to "other" Black folks who choose to live a different lifestyle and behave a certain way.

Is there a Black rule book I have not read? Where is the rule saying Black folks cannot have nice things or have high standards? And does it say in this invisible rule book that Black folks who don't like or have nice things, or who don't have high standards, are inferior to or "less than" than those who do? Than the bourgeois? We are oppressed not only by the labels non-Black folks put on us, but also by the labels we put on each other.

These labels and their use are the master's tools; they are Weapons of Whiteness wielded by Black folks to inflict the gray version of white terrorism and anti-blackness against one another. I call it "Gray Violence." It's when Black people use the thoughts, behaviors, and actions of whiteness to cause harm to their fellow Black people. This type of violence is no less vicious than white violence, and it often cuts deeper because we do not expect to be harmed by our own. Although painful, we have become accustomed to white folks causing intentional and unconscious harm; we just expect them to show up and behave in certain toxic ways. But even though you may have been harmed by Black folks in the past, when it happens again, the pain just hits you differently. We are often shocked by it, although we shouldn't be. We tend to hold grudges against each other longer than we do with white folks. And we hold them deeply and personally. We can be extremely unforgiving of Black folks who harm us.

I get it. I completely understand why we do that, and I believe there are two reasons for it. The first is we have been master-fully manipulated, at a microscopic level, into the insidious indoctrination of self-hatred and anti-blackness. The way we harm each other is both nefarious and nuanced. And unless we are doing our own personal dismantling of this self-hatred, we will continue to violate and oppress each other by weaponizing our hierarchical privileges while in pursuit of fool's gold.

Fool's gold is the second reason we are deeply unforgiving of the harm caused by our fellow Black folks. In our persistent and often unconscious pursuit of fool's gold, we seek to be like whiteness, to be approved by whiteness, and/or to have what whiteness has. Even the most woke of the woke chases fool's gold in some way. The quest often looks very similar to how whiteness operates and dominates, which is to strategically, systematically, and systemically control how Black people think, behave, engage, live, and die. That's it. Since 1619 until today, that is the primary function of whiteness in the lives of Black folks. This is especially true for the descendants of enslaved Africans.

Let me repeat this point: *the core intention of toxic whiteness in the lives of Black people is to control how Black people think, behave, engage, live, and die.* That means controlling what Black folks learn through the racist school system. It means controlling the narrative about Black folks in the media. It means controlling where in a city Black folks live and determining what type of housing accommodations we "deserve." It means controlling whether Black folks get loans from banks and the size of those loans. It means controlling

CHAPTER FIVE | THE MASTER'S TOOLS

what jobs Black folks get and how much money we make. It means controlling Black folks' quality of life, how we leisure, and determining what we have access to. And finally (even though there is much more), it means controlling what Black folks buy and what we eat.

Can you name one thing whiteness does not control in your life? And if you can name more than one, that is remarkable! I would ask you to dig deeper into whether you truly control the things you named. For example, maybe you think you control whom you worship and/or to whom you pray. There's some choice on your part, for sure. But if you go into public spaces and openly confess who or what you believe in, what does whiteness say or do about it? How does the violent and oppressive *White Gaze* (a Weapon of Whiteness) respond to your declaration of sovereignty? Does it limit you in any capacity? Does it determine how others respond to you or treat you? Does it determine whether you're worthy of dignity, respect, protection, and safety?

Examining whether you really have autonomy in how you move through the world, in what you believe, and in how others regard you is necessary so you can see how much control whiteness has over your life. I encourage you to list all the ways in which you believe yourself to be free from the control of whiteness, so you can determine your actual level of freedom and do whatever's necessary to become truly free from the White Gaze. The White Gaze is perhaps the master's most powerful and oppressive tool.

So, what does the White Gaze have to do with you? When you police other Black folks' thoughts, behaviors, actions, and choices, you are essentially doing the work of the master. In fact, you are operating like a plantation overseer—you are doing the dirty work for the master, but not gaining anything but false pride and a few good-negro cookies. When we use class, ethnicity, hair texture, skin color, education levels, and other identifiers to determine which Black folks we honor, serve, include, protect, support, and listen to, we are "overseeing" their blackness; thus, we're controlling it and oppressing them. This behavior is no different from white folks casting their White Gaze upon us.

One way I describe this Gray Violence is like this: when white folks use Weapons of Whiteness against us, they shoot us with full metal jacket (solid tip) bullets to wound or kill us. When Black folks use Weapons of Whiteness against us, they shoot us with hollow-point bullets, the kind that pierce our flesh and shred and tear up shit on the inside. Same weapons. Same master's tools. Closer range. A more intimate, unexpected, and painful experience. Wielding our so-called privileges against one another is how we chase the fool's gold and do the master's violent work. And often we do it so well the master doesn't have to lift a finger while we add bricks to his house. We too attack Black bodies: personally, socially, legally, and structurally. That is anti-blackness.

When Black folks use the master's tools against each other, we don't break down the system of white terrorism; instead, we add another oppressive brick to the master's house. At the end of the day, none of your hierarchical privileges have any real power. They may provide you with a temporary gain over your fellow Black folks, yet in the grand scheme of things, toxic and violent whiteness doesn't care how many degrees you have, how much money is in your bank account, or what kind of car you drive. Toxic whiteness (aka white terrorism) is obsessed with one thing and one thing only: the color of your skin. Not even your ethnicity, just your skin color. And it doesn't matter if your skin is honey-kissed, cocoa brown, midnight black, or caramel swirl. What matters is your skin ain't white. That's it. Period't. Toxic whiteness couldn't care less whether you are Afro-Latina, biracial, or Blackity-Black. And although these "so-called" privileges we have cause real harm and perpetrate oppression upon each other, they are not real to white folks. Blackness, however, they define it, is all they care about, and the fact you're NOT white determines how they perceive and treat you.

Audre Lorde is right when she says, "The master's tools will never dismantle the master's house." The master's toolbox of treachery has an endless supply of Weapons of Whiteness we access and use to marginalize, criminalize, and villainize other Black bodies. We not only use these weapons for personal attacks, but also for professional assassinations. It's inevitable to encounter Beckys and Karens on the job wielding their weapons, but it's startling and disheartening when Black folks take on Becky's and Brad's roles to bash you, defame your character, and sabotage your success. Unfortunately, I have encountered these types of people at every job I've had, and I'm sure you've had run-ins with them too. Beckery and Bradery (particular flavors of white woman violence and white man violence; described in the next chapter) are some helluva drugs.

This kind of violence is intoxicating, and I believe it is a form of addiction. I believe when folks consciously enact the violent whiteness of Beckery and Bradery, they enjoy it. It makes them feel good. Creating and participating in conflict and chaos is personally fulfilling to them. In my work as a therapist, I have witnessed these types of thrill-seeking, chaos-creating behaviors in past clients, and when I have asked them why they engage in such behaviors, they say exactly what I just said: doing so makes them feel good, it gives them a rush, and they enjoy it. What's to enjoy about destroying someone or their livelihood? A better question is, why do folks enjoy creating chaos?

What I have come to understand from my work as a mental health professional are a few real reasons why folks love to create chaos, and why they thrive in it. This maladaptive behavior has become part of their life story. And in most cases, they grew up in an environment where there was a lot of chaos. Fighting. Arguing. In some cases, domestic violence and/or addiction were also present in the household. Chaos became the norm. It became a part of not only their life story, but also their personal narrative. In other words, their self-identity.

The stories we create for ourselves and how we define our self-identity become the script from which we live, and that script determines who and what we either call into our lives or prevent from coming into our lives. You may or may not be responsible for the chaos in your childhood environment, but you are responsible for the chaos in your life today. I also believe failure to recognize your chaos, the story you are living out, the narrative in which you operate, and the identity you've defined for yourself plays a significant role in how you discharge the Weapons of Whiteness as anti-blackness against other Black people. These factors are also instrumental in how much Beckery or Bradery you wield against your fellow Black folks.

LAY DOWN YOUR WEAPONS

WHITE GAZE: When white folks stare at Black and Brown folks with violent curiosity, lust, and/or disgust. Also, when white folks snoop into Black spaces to consume Black thoughts, ideas, and culture.

How do you gaze at other Black people with disgust or dislike? How are you judging them?

_____

_____

_____

_____

WHITE COLLUSION: When white folks willingly or unknowingly co-conspire with white terrorism and racism at the expense of Black and Brown folks. Also, when white folks choose white comfort over justice and equity for nonwhite people.

How are you colluding with whiteness to harm Black people? How are you keeping yourself comfortable versus speaking up for Black people?

_____

_____

_____

_____

WHITE GATEKEEPING: When white folks assume false authority on what Black and Brown folks can or cannot access and do.

What "types" of Black people are you gatekeeping for or against? What qualifiers or criteria are you using to exclude and deny access to other Black people? Why?

_____

_____

_____

_____

WE HAVE TO CONSCIOUSLY STUDY HOW TO BE TENDER WITH EACH OTHER UNTIL IT BECOMES A HABIT.

AUDRE LORDE

CHAPTER
SIX

BLACK BECKYS AND BRADS

We don't have to like each other to love one another.
Catrice M. Jackson

Not all Beckys and Brads are white! There are lots of Brown ones. And unfortunately, some Black ones too! Yes, I need to go there. So here we go! Let's start at the beginning by defining what a Becky is. In my book *The Becky Code*, I describe Becky as a white woman who weaponizes her whiteness to racially violate and oppress Black and Brown folks. She is defensive, emotionally brittle, and spiritually exhausting, and she will suck the life out of you. Becky will always center whiteness, and she will use her whiteness and proximity to the master (white men and the system of white terrorism) to cause racist harm. I call this violent way of engaging "Beckery" and "Beckyism" (and when white men engage in it, I call it "Bradery"). In *The Becky Code,* I define Beckyism as follows:

> Beckyism is the violent and oppressive way in which white women who are not doing any personal anti-racism work will engage with women of color. As a result of white supremacy and white privilege, white women believe they can say and do anything they want when engaging with black, brown, Native, and Indigenous women without

suffering any consequences. Beckyism is dismissive, accusatory, and oppressive, and Becky works to violate, silence, and marginalize women of color. This is what white women do to black, brown, Native, and Indigenous women all the time. This is what Becky does. The emotionally abusive behaviors I describe above are toxic to your well-being, and they are what I call Beckery!

—Catrice M. Jackson, *The Becky Code*

Beckys are oblivious, obnoxious, and oppressive. They view the world through a white supremacist lens that is invalidating, insulting, and assaultive. Beckery is conscious, unconscious, and insidious. Some Beckys know exactly what they are doing, and others act out their violence through willful ignorance. Either way, Beckyism is designed to invade and violate your psyche, space, peace, and joy. And Beckyism has four clear goals, the Four D's I discussed in Chapter 1: to *deny* your lived experience, to *defend* white terroristic violence, to *derail* any conversations about white violence, and to *destroy* you mentally and emotionally.

I know you have experienced Beckery and Bradery from *white folks*, but let's switch gears: have you ever experienced this kind of behavior from *Black folks*? I have. And I have been this kind of Black Becky too. Let's first talk about what the Black Becky and Black Brad experience looks like on the receiving end. The root cause of this violence is the same as it is for white people: the generations of indoctrination into white terrorism. Black parents and caregivers don't necessarily sit down with a lesson plan and teach these violent thoughts and behaviors;

instead, we learn to embody them vicariously through our home environments. And it does not matter if the home is your parent's home, your auntie's or grandparent's home, or a foster home—I'm talking about the spaces and places where you were raised.

The conditioning that takes place becomes a double-edged sword. We not only learn about the fallacy of white supremacy, we also learn that proximity to whiteness is powerful, and it is manifested as anti-blackness and self-hatred. We learn the more we look like and behave like white folks, the "better" we are. We learn and believe light-skinned folks have more rights to resources and opportunities. And when we learn these lessons, we internalize that Black folks who are the furthest from whiteness (darker-skinned Black folks, primarily) are inferior and undeserving. In other words, whiteness is using Black bodies to harm other Black bodies.

If white folks were suddenly and magically unable to cause racist harm, Black folks would still be a significant detriment to Black people's mental and emotional health. When we pick up Weapons of Whiteness internalized as anti-blackness, our behavior is like Becky's and Brad's, with the same goals of *denying* another Black person's lived experience, *defending* our anti-blackness, *derailing* conversations about our anti-black violence, and *destroying* each other mentally and emotionally. These goals are the same Four D's that I described earlier (and in *The Becky Code*): deny, defend, derail, and destroy.

Although this chapter emphasizes the psychology of Becky (which I call "Beckyology"), the behaviors described are fitting for Black men too. That's because gender has very little to do with the core of anti-blackness, which stems from internalized self-hatred and metabolized oppression. In other words, just as Weapons of Whiteness (the master's tools) can be wielded by anyone who is white, these same internalized weapons can be used by all Black folks to cause harm to other Black folks.

I want you to think deeply about how the previous paragraph began. Go back and read it again. *White terrorism is so pervasive and virulent that it will survive within the Black community even if the white host dies.* That's deep and dangerous. It is critically important that we starve this disease within ourselves; it must die where it exists in each of us, and we must stop passing it on to future generations. This is one way we will survive and thrive in the face of systemic white terrorism.

I could provide many examples of what Beckyism in Black bodies looks like. Instead, I want you to think about what you have read so far about Weapons of Whiteness and then consider how you have used those same weapons against other Black people. Are you able to make a connection between your own internalized anti-blackness and how you have treated the Black people you know and engage with? Now, don't get me wrong. Not every disagreement, or negative feeling, thought, or behavior toward another Black person is the result of anti-blackness. Sometimes personalities clash. Sometimes you just do not like a person, and sometimes Black folks cause you harm.

It is also important that I make the following points for lighter-skinned or white-passing Black people. First and most important, if you believe you are experiencing anti-blackness from a darker-skinned Black person, I challenge you to examine why that might be happening. Is their negative or hurtful response to you because of some form of exclusion and/or anti-blackness you have shown them, whether consciously or unconsciously? It is likely this is the case. Second, even if you have not personally done something anti-black to them, someone lighter-skinned like you has, and the darker-skinned person is probably responding to past acts of anti-black violence and trauma. This is not always what is going on, but as I said, it is highly likely.

Those of you who are lighter-skinned might be thinking this response by darker-skinned folks is unfair and unreasonable. I get it. I understand because I used to believe this too. Just like white folks, we light-skinned folks think we are exceptional. And although it is true we are being punished or judged by white people because of the color of our skin, there is also historical evidence that shows we have used our proximity to whiteness and light-skinned privilege as weapons against darker-skinned Black people in various forms. It was light-skinned folks, according to oral history, who created the Brown Paper Bag Test to discriminate against darker-skinned people. If someone's skin was darker than the paper bag, they would be denied access, permission, and privileges to exclusive spaces and places. It was also light-skinned folks who made the distinction about good hair versus bad hair as another way to practice anti-blackness while chasing the master's fool's gold.

These two acts of violence are part of what we know as colorism. And while colorism is only one of the master's tools we use to perpetrate anti-blackness against one another, I believe it is a fundamental part of anti-black racism and discrimination within the Black community and other communities of color. Make no mistake, all the tools are a version of toxic whiteness, and when we use them against one another, we are committing Gray Violence. As a reminder, I defined Gray Violence in the previous chapter as "...when Black people use the thoughts, behaviors, and actions of whiteness to cause harm to fellow Black people." Gray Violence is simply Beckery in a Black body.

Let me use three classic BECKYS, defined in detail in *The Becky Code*, to further illustrate how Beckery is manifested through anti-blackness: Miss Anne, Becky, and Rachel Dolezal. Let's start with Miss Anne because she's unforgettable! She is arrogant, uppity, and condescending. She may show up as prim and proper, snooty and slick with her racist undertones, and she has no problem letting you know she has a problem with you. I liken Miss Anne to the character Miss Millie from *The Color Purple*. Miss Anne is often an older woman who has no filter, and she will stare you up and down for no reason with the White Gaze. She will turn her nose up at you because she thinks you are beneath her. This type of Becky is easy to spot because her racism is unapologetic and explicit; her problematic behavior is in plain sight.

The Black Miss Anne is no different. I have been her, and I have been on the receiving end of her ant-black violence. I cannot count the times I have thought I am better than other Black folks. I have consciously and unconsciously launched my Weapons of Whiteness in the form of thinking certain Black folks were "ghetto" and a disgrace to the Black race. I have judged other Black folks for their use of language; I have thought of their vernacular as lazy, ignorant, and embarrassing. I have distanced myself from Black folks who are loud and indignant in social settings to prove I am "not like them." I was surely trying to appease and comfort the White Gaze by behaving in such a pseudo-exceptional way. And as much as I hate to admit it, there were times when I was afraid of my own people. I was nervous to be around too many loud Black folks and anxious about being in the "hood." I have turned my nose up at other Black folks simply because, for whatever reason, I thought I was above them. I was in pursuit of the master's fool's gold. I used all my hierarchical privileges to disenfranchise and marginalize Black folks, especially those who were darker-skinned than I am. And I justified all this violence by the lie white folks tell and indoctrinate us with: we should pull ourselves up by our bootstraps to be better and have more. I used to be embarrassed by these truths, but now I embrace them, own them, and work to eradicate my own anti-blackness. Black Miss Anne's harm is not different from white Miss Anne's, but it is more intimate and devastating.

I have shown up as Black Miss Anne in more ways than expressed, I'm sure, and I've been treated the same way by other Black Miss Annes. I've been excluded from certain Black cliques, ignored and silenced by Black folks who believed they were better than I am, and looked down on by folks you might call "the Black elite." I have also been deemed "not Black enough" because my skin is lighter than some Black folks.

This left me wandering somewhere in the middle of nowhere as I tried to figure out what being "Black enough" really meant, while harming other Black folks by questioning their blackness. Now if that shit doesn't sound like a damn episode of *The Twilight Zone*, I don't know what does. And if you are honest, you can probably see yourself wandering and

CHAPTER SIX | BLACK BECKYS AND BRADS

harming too. Because none of us Black folks have it all figured out, nor have we mastered how to not be anti-black.

We all are chasing the master's fool's gold in some way, whether we are cognizant of it or not. Although we despise the truth that we've been infected with the virus of toxic whiteness, my hope for you is you'll own it, examine it, and begin to disinfect yourself from this virus and all the insidious ways it permeates your psyche and way of being in the world. This is our work to do. To rid ourselves of the Beckery that lives within us, in the places we cannot see at first glance.

I remember in my early years of entrepreneurship, I would eagerly seek guidance and support from Black women who I thought were successful entrepreneurs. And let me tell you, they rarely offered any substantial advice for success. This was back during the social media guru days, about ten years ago, when everybody and they mama was chasing the fool's gold flavor of "make six figures." Hell, I was trying to figure out how I too could become a six-figure earner. I hate to say it, but many of the Black women "six-figure" earners would not give me the time of day. Unless, of course, I paid for their "high-end" coaching course. I surely would have, but I didn't have the funds.

Let me just say the first eight years or so of my entrepreneurial journey lacked significant colleague support and Black-woman sisterhood. I can't say for sure why I wasn't able to garner the support of my Black sisters, but I'm confident in my belief they were too busy dismissing Black folks who had not yet arrived and stepping on the backs of Black folks in hot pursuit of fool's gold. How do I know? Because that is what whiteness teaches us. I know, because I would do the same violent shit to Black women who had not yet arrived where I thought I was on the fake-ass success ladder. It is all a vicious cycle of violence we learned from the creators of the cycle. Ain't nothing but colonizers' mindset.

Over the past ten years, I have dedicated myself to the undoing of this unwarranted spitefulness, and I am currently on a journey of unlearning the ways in which I am still intoxicated by the insidious destructiveness of whiteness. I know it is easy for you and me to believe we are "woke" and disinfected, but we are not. Whiteness is so slick, sneaky, and deceptive that we do not always realize how much of it we breathe in every day. It is like we're sitting in a running car in a closed garage breathing in the toxic and deadly fumes of carbon monoxide, but we don't think we're even in the car. I believe even the most wokest-of woke, Blackity-pro-black Black folks still inhale the ferocious fumes of toxic whiteness. After all, it's in the air we breathe; toxic whiteness is ubiquitous. It is universal. Name a place in the world where the infectious virus of whiteness is not in some way permeating how Black and Brown people engage with each other. Even Mother Africa cannot escape the grip that whiteness has on its richness.

The toxic whiteness within is often hard to identify, especially when it hides behind the mask of wokeness, solidarity, and "we all we got." Much like Becky and her Beckyism, it's often hiding in plain sight, yet we are blinded by Black folks who perform their blackness but who are not working on eradicating their anti-blackness. Fortunately, a Becky (or Brad) can't hide her Beckery (or Bradery) for long. With the right trigger, they will expose the anti-blackness behind the mask.

CHAPTER SIX | BLACK BECKYS AND BRADS

The Becky you will encounter most often is just called "Becky." This white woman will be the one who is hard to detect as a racist because she thinks she is progressive, liberal, and "one of the good ones." Becky is your typical, often mediocre, on the low, "I'm not racist" racist white woman who is clueless about her white woman privilege and "modern-day" (aka subtle) racism. Becky tends to believe that she is a white woman who "gets it" (racism), and she will proudly tell you about all the good white things she believes and has done in her lifetime. She'll make sure you know that her best friend (now in high school or college) is Black, or perhaps she's married to a Black person, or her children or nieces and nephews are biracial, aka half-Black. In other words, she will tell you all the reasons she is NOT racist. Reasons I am sure you've heard a million times before, right? Predictable and exhausting! And Becky truly believes she knows more about racism and oppression than you do. She has read some books, watched a few documentaries, and possibly has participated in diversity training. Oblivious to what racism really is and to her own racism, she often believes she is an exceptional white woman.

Becky is also known for tone policing you, interrupting you, talking over you, reaching over you, and if given the chance, she will speak for you. She asks a lot of questions and expects answers, she likes to play devil's advocate, and if you confront her racism, she'll feel attacked and declare you are the racist who is just trying to shame her. Becky is your classic, textbook version of white woman violence.

As I said at the beginning of this chapter, not all Beckys are white. I have seen Beckery show up in all different shades and bodies including Black ones. Just like white Beckys, Black

Beckys (and Black Brads) are the type of people you will encounter most often. Black Becky's anti-blackness may not be overt; it more likely lurks under the surface of her Black Girl Magic. She too is one who believes she is not anti-black, and she will go above and beyond to prove how Black she is, while minimizing and condemning other folks' blackness.

One of the primary ways that Black Beckys show their anti-blackness is by how much and how often they cape for white folks. In the past, I certainly used the phrase "not all white people." Especially during my younger days of running ragged while chasing fool's gold, I believed there were some good white folks out there. And although I didn't majorly cape for them, I still caped for them a bit by defending them when other Black folks would point out their racism. I always knew all white folks are racist, and looking back, I am sure when I came to their defense, it was more a case of me protecting my bread and butter. My defense of them usually occurred in the workplace, and as you know, you've got to make sure them white folks don't mess with your bread. I used to see other Black women also behave this way in the workplace, but now that I am an entrepreneur, I frequently see it in online spaces.

Watching Black folks defend and cape for white folks is beyond cringeworthy! It is truly pathetic and quite despicable to see a Black person come for another Black person to save Becky. I used to argue and debate about this tactic online much more than I do now. When I see Black Becky's white savior cape come out, I get to stepping real quick, because not only is it an exhausting exchange, it's also a lose-lose situation. When Black folks are committed to defending Becky and Brad, there is not much you can do to convince them to stop, because they are in hot, relentless pursuit of that fool's gold. And it must be said, quite often a Black person who capes for Becky or Brad is dating, sleeping with, or is married to a Becky or a Brad. I know. That's a generalized statement. One with a lot of truth to it.

When I think back to the Black Beckys who have come for me in the last few years, they have all fit that description. They usually come to tell me how I am not being fair to white folks or how their special white person is different from other white people. They believe I am being too harsh to white folks and that I don't give them the opportunity for reconciliation and redemption. And if a Black Becky doesn't come for me directly, she is salty in her engagements with me, and/or she throws shade at me or my work because she's pissed I'm shining the light of truth on her special white person. And guess what, IDGAF. I really don't. I will always speak the truth, even if it hurts.

I believe I can call a thing a thing when calling out or pointing out white people's anti-blackness and white terrorism, and I can do so without coddling them or hating them. That is what I do. Unapologetically, and with no filter. I realize this makes *some* Black people uncomfortable, and often their discomfort turns into making me the aggressor for refusing to allow white folks to harm or oppress me or other Black folks. Although this response from Black folks is startling at first, I understand why they do it.

A perfect example of this caping for white folks is happening as I write this chapter. I made a post on Facebook a few days ago about how white folks should not lead discussions or training about racism, and a Black woman is on the post lecturing me about how "not all white people" are bad and how we "need" them to end white terrorism. She is going hard in her defense of those exceptional white folks who deserve consideration, she is antagonizing Black women in the thread, and she is suggesting I should give some white folks a pass. Le sigh... What I realize in this situation is that something I said pushed her "we need white saviors" button and triggered her subconscious need for white approval. She may not see that, but it is clear. What other reasons are possible for her defense of white folks? What is the point and endgame of arguing with another Black woman about the significance of a few good white folks? Welp. I discovered she is married to a white man. And yes, I know that not all Black folks in relationships with white folks are like this, but it is common.

I am aware there have been some white folks who have done good things for Black folks, and there are those who stand up against racial injustice. I think most Black folks are aware of the white folks who are trying to do the right thing for Black lives. Yet to try to shove these rare folks down another Black person's throat is unnecessary and violent.

It is my belief white folks should do their own personal anti-racism work while encouraging other white folks to get on their anti-racism journey. I believe those are the two most important actions white folks can take: do their own work and get other white folks to do theirs. Oh, and pay reparations. But I will never agree to white folks leading discussions about racism or formally teaching anything that has to do with anti-racism and white terrorism. Especially if they are socially or financially profiting from educating.

CHAPTER SIX | BLACK BECKYS AND BRADS

In fact, I believe it is white folks' responsibility to lead other white folks to Black and Brown educators who are willing to do the hard, laborious work of educating white folks. I stand in agreement with Glenn E. Martin, who says, "Those closest to the problem are closest to the solution." It is Black and Brown folks who experience the problem of whiteness; therefore, they have the solutions to end white terrorism, not white folks who refuse to—or are incapable of—seeing their own racist blind spots.

Finally, let's talk about the most horrendous Becky of all. Rachel Dolezal Becky! She is a combination of different attributes from many types of Becky; this is her description from *The Becky Code*:

> Whew chile! She is the absolute worst and the one that I have zero tolerance for. I like to call this type of Becky Ole-Thieving-Ass Becky: A Becky who rapes and robs the culture of black people to create an identity so she can feel alive inside. She's also a disastrous and dangerous blend of Wanna-Be-Black-Becky, Get-On-Your-Nerves Becky, Talk-Too-Damn-Much Becky and Know-It-All Becky, and she will exhaust the hell out of you. If Trans-Racial were a real thing, Rachel Dolezal Becky would be the poster child. Rachel Dolezal Becky is the worst kind of Becky, the most violent Becky of all. Rachel takes Wanna-Be-Black Becky to the ultimate offense. She thinks she is black, wants to be black, appropriates the culture of blackness and deeply craves being accepted by black folks, especially black women. This Becky perpetrates fraudulent behavior on the daily and there is absolutely no shame in

her fake-ass game. She loves her some black people, fetishizes all forms of blackness and has mastered AAVE so well that if you couldn't see her, you'd swear you were talking to a black woman. Rachel Dolezal Becky works my nerves!

—Catrice M. Jackson, *The Becky Code*

Rachel Dolezal is still out here claiming blackness and declaring she is transracial. What? What does that even mean? I watched a recent video clip where she was being interviewed about reparations by a Black man. He asked her if and when reparations are paid, whether she thought she should receive them or not. She said, "No, because I'm not Black, I'm transracial." What the hell! That makes absolutely no sense at all. Rachel Dolezal is clearly confused. I am beginning to think she really believes she is a Black woman trapped in a white body. Anyway, enough about that Ole-Thieving-Ass Becky.

So how do Black women and men show up like Rachel Dolezal today? Black Rachels (and Black Richards) do not want to be Black, or they want to be as "white" as possible. And just like Rachel's wanna-be-Black wish is exaggerated, Black Rachel's and Black Richard's wanna-be-white wishes are exaggerated. In his book The Souls of Black Folks, W.E.B Du Bois described the phenomenon of what he termed "double consciousness" within Black folks as a *"peculiar sensation upon which Double Consciousness is the sense of always looking at one's self through the eyes of others, of measuring one's soul by the tape of a world that looks on in amused contempt and pity."*

In my opinion, Black Rachels and Black Richards are in a constant state of double consciousness. I cannot imagine what it must be like for them to look in the mirror and see a Black body but feel like they are white on the inside. And what does it even mean to "feel" white on the inside?

What I can say is this conflict is an extraordinary case of cognitive dissonance. In simple terms, cognitive dissonance is like double consciousness, in that there is a conflict of thought happening. When cognitive dissonance occurs, a person thinks two or more contradicting thoughts, and in the case of Black Rachels and Black Richards, the thoughts may sound like, "I don't like my blackness" and "I can never be white." There is clearly a lot of disconnection and misalignment for these people. When someone is experiencing cognitive dissonance, they will do one of two things: they will either ignore the conflicting thoughts (reject reality) and behave in the way that is the least emotionally stressful, or they will be receptive to new information and facts that allow them to create inner harmony between their thoughts and behavior. For the purpose of diving a bit deeper here, I'll use a hypothetical Black man named George to further illustrate my point.

Let's say George is a very dark-skinned man that was teased and called derogatory names due to his skin color throughout his childhood. Subsequently, George develops a color complex and internalizes the anti-black attacks against him. He starts to hate being Black, despises his skin color, and distances himself from Black people and Black culture. Over the years, his resentment of his blackness deepens and expands to the point where he can see beauty, power, and opportunities only within whiteness. George has not openly said he hates his blackness, but subconsciously he increases his proximity to whiteness. He dates white women exclusively (even though his mama is Black), he hangs out in places that are predominantly white, and most of his friends are white. And he begins to love what white folks love, while growing further away from his blackness, his Black family, and anything that resembles "blackness."

George starts chasing fool's gold, and he consciously and unconsciously starts using Weapons of Whiteness against Black folks he engages with. Some folks would call this type of person an Oreo: Black on the outside and white on the inside. Obviously, George is experiencing a conflict—not only in thought and behavior, but also between reality and fantasy. As much as George tries to be white, he stares at a Black face in the mirror every day. Therefore, he is experiencing double consciousness and cognitive dissonance.

George is not in alignment. He could try to reconcile his conflict and lack of inner harmony by ignoring or devaluing the truth that he can never be white, associating with other Black folks who look and think like he does, and avoiding contact with Black folks who will burst his bubble of dissonance with the truth. But if George continues with this type of thinking and behaving, he will remain in inner conflict, which creates tension, dissatisfaction, and a sense of emptiness. Because no matter how hard George tries to be white, he will never be accepted by the white collective. No matter how fast he chases the fool's gold, he will never obtain it. And no matter how much George disassociates from blackness, he will never escape his Black skin. Black Rachel Dolezal Beckys are consumed with whiteness. They fetishize and try to mimic whiteness, thus almost completely abandoning their blackness, while desperately trying to secure their spot in Massa's big house.

And even with a secured spot, George will never be seen or treated like a white person. Not even by those "good, liberal, progressive, I-don't-see-color" white folks. And not even the ones he sleeps with. In fact, the white Becky he ends up marrying (or being in a relationship with) will kill him at close range with a full and plentiful arsenal of Weapons of Whiteness. George will emotionally die in the Sunken Place. And the only way he may survive is if his Becky commits to life-long anti-racist work, and even then, she will always be infected with toxic whiteness.

George is a Black Richard, and he is no different than a Rachel Dolezal Becky. He lives in a false reality and causes harm to himself and others using Weapons of Whiteness and anti-blackness. George's thirst for white acceptance and hunger for fool's gold will cause him to abandon his blackness, turn his nose up at Black folks, and sacrifice his true self to increase his proximity to whiteness.

George has another option, though: he can decide to look in the mirror and see the beauty, power, and value in his Black skin. He can heal his childhood wounds caused by anti-blackness. He can reconnect to his blackness and its rich and resourceful culture. He can stop chasing the white man's fool's gold and tap into the riches within himself. He can embrace what it means to be Black on his own terms. He can love, adore, and honor the Black skin he lives in. He can get back into alignment and stop the inner chaos and conflict. He can be his true self by returning to the sovereignty and wholeness of being proud of his blackness and all that it means for him. This is how George can reconcile his cognitive dissonance and be of ONE consciousness.

George may be a hypothetical person, but believe me, there are plenty of real Georges and Ginas in the world who live a life like the one I have described. And make no mistake about it, these Georges and Ginas cause harm to other Black folks by intentionally and unintentionally wielding their Weapons of Whiteness and attacking with anti-blackness.

The truth is, we all have some Becky or Brad within us. None of us are immune to the lethal infection of toxic whiteness. And if we are unwilling to tell the truth about our version of Beckery or Bradery, we will continue to harm and oppress each other. When we pick up the master's tools to use against one another, it is guaranteed we do so with the same intentions as when white folks use them: to deny, defend, derail, and destroy. The Four D's are destructive and deadly no matter who uses them. And so, the ultimate question is, what kind of Becky or Brad lives inside you? Are you willing to go down deep into the dungeon of your heart to find your Weapons of Whiteness? Are you willing to dig up your anti-blackness to analyze and eradicate it? Are you willing to realize you are never going to obtain fool's gold? And are you willing to stop stepping on the backs of other Black folks in pursuit of a spot in the master's house?

We must deeply believe what Audre Lorde says about the master's tools not dismantling the master's house. And not only believe it, but also embody her teachings about ending oppression against each other. She was right then, and she is right now.

LAY DOWN YOUR WEAPONS

WHITE FETISHIZATION: When white folks objectify, glorify, consume, and dehumanize the Black body for profit and pleasure.

How are you dehumanizing the Black body for pleasure or profit?

_____

_____

_____

_____

WHITE CONSUMPTION: When white folks consume blackness and Black and Brown people's energy and space for their own personal gain.

Are there ways in which you are using someone else's blackness for personal gain?

_____

_____

_____

_____

WHITE LARCENY: When white folks increase their proximity to Black and Brown folks and their cultures to appropriate, rape, rob, and steal from nonwhite folks.

Are there ways in which you are stealing from other Black people for personal gain?

_____

_____

_____

_____

WE CANNOT LOVE "OUR PEOPLE" UNLESS WE LOVE EACH OF US OURSELVES, UNLESS I LOVE EACH PIECE OF MYSELF, THOSE I WISH TO KEEP AND THOSE I WISH TO CHANGE—FOR SURVIVAL IS THE ABILITY TO ENCOMPASS DIFFERENCE, TO ENCOMPASS CHANGE WITHOUT DESTRUCTION.

AUDRE LORDE
I AM YOUR SISTER: COLLECTED AND UNPUBLISHED WRITINGS

CHAPTER SEVEN

BOUNTY HUNTERS

> Whiteness is so slick it will have you hating and hunting your own people.
>
> Catrice M. Jackson

Before the end of the United States Civil War, bounty hunters were people emboldened by legalized kidnapping to stalk Black enslaved bodies (aka "property") and return them to the master's house of horror by any means necessary. When enslaved Black folks escaped the torture and degradation of plantation captivity, bounties were placed on their heads, and lynch mobs mounted up to monetize their disregard for blackness. Usually white folks were the headhunters; however, there were times when Black folks were in cahoots with white bounty hunters, and other times when Black headhunters were leading the charge in the pursuit of runaway, aka fugitive, slaves.

Who sanctioned this evil activity? Article 4, Section 2, Clause 3 of the original version of the U.S. Constitution stated that escaped enslaved people were to be returned. But that was not enough for the Constitution's sinister authors; the Fugitive Slave Act of 1793 was enacted to enforce the clause, and the Fugitive Slave Act of 1850 was enacted to enforce it in even stronger terms. This second Act of 1850 required the U.S. government to participate in the recapturing of runaway slaves. Listen to that again. Federal officers were *required by law* to actively assist with the repossession of a human being! That is pure sick evil and shows you the authors of the Act were just as vile as the authors of the Constitution. It is no surprise, though. The founding terrorists (they ain't my damn forefathers!) built the national government of the United States and its fundamental laws on inhumanity, savagery, and apathy for Black lives. It is unconscionable what enslaved Africans and Black folks endured during these horrific moments. But then again, the terror and horror are still a daily reality for us.

According to the 1860 census, there were approximately four million enslaved Africans in the United States. Four million. And that may not even be an accurate count, because white historians have proven they omit the truth about the travesty of chattel slavery. How can you trust the recordkeeping of folks who would brutally and inhumanely enslave Black bodies for pleasure and profit? Regardless of this number's accuracy, I wonder how many enslaved Africans tried to escape, and how often they were recaptured due to the assistance of other Black folks. Headhunters. When I think deeply about this, it truly saddens me to know we still hunt each other, to know we spend wasted energy on coming for one another, and often for the pettiest of reasons. Unfortunately, these Black vendettas are a manifestation of toxic whiteness. This is the toxicity we must work to rid ourselves of every day we breathe.

Did you know that in 1851, an American doctor named Samuel Cartwright theorized that enslaved Black people who tried to escape were mentally ill? He called the "disorder" drapetomania, an uncontrollable and insane impulse to wander. (Notice that Cartwright came up with this garbage of pseudoscience shortly after the passing of the Fugitive Slave Act.) Even more sickening were Cartwright's suggestions for the cure! He believed if masters treated the enslaved more like children, they would be deterred from running away—yet he also believed masters who treated the enslaved with any sort of kindness, generosity, or humanity caused drapetomania. Cartwright further advised that when the enslaved sulked, it meant they were contemplating their escape. One remedy for this malady was to cut off their big toes so they could not leave, and he also recommended "whipping the devil" out of them so they would return to their subservient and submissive demeanors.

And of course, many of Cartwright's theories were derived from a sick and twisted manipulation of Bible scripture; he claimed it was God's will for Black people to be enslaved and to be subservient to their masters. What a violent crock of shit! Anyone in their right mind would realize this line of psychotic thinking was a treacherous lie. Look closely at the fundamental pathology in such a claim. Only folks suffering from a mental illness would concur with this barbaric thought pattern.

Sadly, this type of sociopathic thought was common during the time of chattel slavery, and still is today. Aggression, narcissism, apathy, grandiosity, shallow emotions, disregard for right and wrong, lack of remorse, and the incapacity for love are the primary, classic character traits of a sociopath. Slave masters, plantation owners, and all those who believed in and/or upheld the captivity, bondage, and brutality of human beings walk in the shoes of a sociopath. I like to say those folks were evil to the core. Yet enslaved Black folks were deemed mentally ill for wanting to escape a forced life of savagery and dehumanization. Doesn't sound at all crazy to me. And although many enslaved Black folks tried to escape, there were even more who chose to stay in bondage. Their reasons for doing so were valid, justifiable, and rational. The price recaptured slaves paid was higher than I can adequately articulate. Castration. Hot-boxing. Boiled in hot sugar. Hung from a tree. Mutilation. Branding. Dismemberment. Rape. Beatings.

And God only knows what other horrific punishments they suffered for seeking their God-given right to be sovereign and free. The threat of those atrocities is enough to explain why some enslaved Black people were afraid to run and instead chose to stay on the plantation. It sounds damn logical to me. What is most disturbing, however, are the Black people who co-conspired and partnered up with white folks to hunt down runaways to return to the plantations, and that they did so for profit.

Sad but true. There have always been Black folks among us willing to be bounty hunters for the beast that literally and spiritually hunts and kills us, both for personal gain and for closer proximity to toxic whiteness. I remember when the movie *Harriet* debuted in 2019, a lot of Black folks were upset and enraged that one of the bounty hunters in the movie was a Black man. Some of them boycotted the movie and expressed their anger on social media. I understood the rage, but I knew that although this man's role in the Harriet Tubman story was vilified, it was the truth. Then and now.

The Black folks who operated in the role of bounty hunter back in the day did so for various reasons. Some did it for mere survival, and others did it for personal profit in the form of goods, resources, and on rare occasions, for their "freedom." And still these hunters exist. After all, it is a truth that each of us has orchestrated and/or participated in the bounty on another Black person's head at least once in our lifetime. I certainly have on more than one occasion. When I took part in intentional headhunting, I felt justified in my actions, and I did not make the connection between my internalized anti-blackness and my Black-body vendettas. Today I see the correlation clearly and am remorseful for the pain I caused.

Like most of the anti-black acts of violence I have discussed in this book, I have not only been a perpetrator of this same type of violence, but I am also a victim/survivor. And perhaps this is true for you too. In my young adulthood years, I did not have the intellectual bandwidth to see this truth of being both a perpetrator and a victim, let alone be able to accurately define it or process it. If I am honest, my awareness has dramatically and steadily increased since my late thirties and has continued with fast-tracked learning that occurs every day I breathe. I do not claim to have all the answers. Just some.

If I had to name the two biggest ways I have been a perpetrator of anti-black violence against other Black folks, they would be wielding the weapons of colorism and respectability. I have shared some examples in earlier chapters. I now have the desire as well as the intellectual and emotional capacity to look at my anti-black oppressive behaviors, name and own them, and work to eliminate them. But sometimes I'm not able to identify my anti-blackness at all because of my own "privileged" lens. This is when my real inner work must begin, when people point out my violence. It's hard to receive such feedback, because by nature we all want to believe we are good people doing our best. The truth is we are good people, and we can always do and be better. But yeah, back in the day, I put bounties on other Black folks' heads for various reasons, including because they did not speak "proper" or they were too "ghetto."

I've frequently seen bounties placed on Black folks by other Black folks in the workplace. You would think we would have a mentality that tells us, "We better stick together or else we will all die in this ocean of white supremacy." Sadly, that was not often the case. I remember working for a non-profit organization that served families with infants and children. Ninety percent of the staff was Black, the other ten percent was made up of NBPOC and white folks, and the children we served were predominantly Black. I was a center manager at the time, and it was the first time I had had a job at a company where most of the staff was Black. I was so thrilled to finally have the opportunity to work with my people. I just knew the experience was going to be less stressful and more rewarding. I started the position wearing rose-colored glasses, and I had blind faith that my fellow Black people would know the struggle of being Black in the workplace, and therefore, we would for the most part get along very well without the oppressive White Gaze. I was excited to not have to minimize my blackness and anticipated being with my people without having to shift.

That optimism and excitement faded immediately on my first day on the job. Literally, on the first day, it was clear that my Black colleagues had all kinds of bounties on each other's heads. I must admit this observation was startling and troubling. Call me naive or whatever. I could not believe what I was seeing, yet it was also so crystal clear.

It was particularly noticeable during a manager's leadership meeting. We were in a large room, in chairs set up in a U-shaped seating arrangement. The meeting space was filled with beautiful artwork and colorful expressions of joy that depicted the love for educating and caring for children. But there was little joyful or loving energy in the room. I sat quietly in deep observation of the interpersonal engagement of my colleagues, who all happened to be Black people. As each one shared an update about what was happening in his or her center, you could have used a knife to slice through the tension, jealousy, and resentment building up in the space. One after another they threw shade, made accusations, rolled their eyes, and tuned each other out, while vying to be heard and to be right.

There was clearly some competition going on. Competition for recognition, rewards, and closer proximity to the whiteness known as senior leadership. I don't have a problem with folks climbing the ladder, but I do have a problem with Black folks stepping on the necks of other Black folks on the climb toward fool's gold. And I had my fair share of problems in my center, with staff cussing out parents, teachers not following lesson plans, and folks doing whatever they wanted. Like seriously, I was blown away by this interaction. I had high hopes and great optimism about finally working with my people. Black people.

It seemed like a lot of this organization's Black employees had bounties out on their Black colleagues; I sensed an "out to get each other for some kind of reward" mentality. I wanted to believe this was a fluke. Just a rare moment at the office, you know. Unfortunately, it was not a fluke; in fact, it was a deeply embedded set of beliefs and behaviors that plagued the organization to the point of eventual closure, officially due to the collective inability to meet the standards and goals set forth by the national governing body. In my opinion, the closure was actually due to white terrorism, which first created the barrel and put Black people in it, and then stood back while Black folks not only clawed at and fought each other trying to get out of the barrel, but also kicked other Black folks down on their climb up.

I did not have this awareness during my time employed there. I was also unaware of how much anti-blackness was lurking underneath my optimistic "I can't wait to work with my people" mentality. I see now what I really wanted was to work with certain kinds of Black people. Respectable Black folks. Professional Black folks. Proper-speaking (aka white-speaking) Black folks. Well-behaved Black folks. Black folks who, like me, were in pursuit of the fool's gold. Essentially, I wanted to work with Black folks who were not too ghetto.

Sigh. There it is. The truth. The horrible, ugly, offensive truth. It took me several years to clearly see my anti-blackness in this situation. And while my revelation was evolving, I made many justifications for my skewed and harmful thoughts about Black people. I believed I was right. I believed I was better than "them" in some ways. I believed I knew the right answers to "their" challenges. I believed I was above and beyond their foolishness, and someday they would finally wake up and realize the truth about their self-sabotaging ways.

Sheesh! Who does this Caucasity sound like? Precisely. It sounds like all the Beckys and Brads who get on our nerves with their white violence. This shit sounds like Karen and nem! And while my truth is sad and sobering, it is real, and perhaps you too are showing up like Becky, Brad, or Karen during your engagements with Black folks, as I described in the previous chapter.

I have yet to meet a Black person who is not in some way clinging to their internalized anti-blackness and causing harm to other Black people, whether they know it or not. This is where we need to be honest with ourselves, not only by exploring the ways in which we cause this harm, but also by making the choice to stop this violence. I have learned a lot about my anti-blackness, and I continue to learn how to consistently hold myself accountable for how I weaponize it. I am a work in progress, and so are you, but only if you are honest and willing to do this critical self-work.

We must stop putting bounties out on each other for being a different kind of Black person. You may not like what I am about to say, but it is the truth. None of us Black folks had a choice in being born Black. We also did not have a choice in who our parents would be. We did not get to choose the complexion of our skin or the texture of our hair. We had no choice in what our facial features or body structure would look like. We did not get to choose our birthplace or the circumstances of our childhood environment. When we were born into this world, we were born Black with no control over our appearance. We did not get to choose what neighborhood we grew up in, or whether we were in a one- or two-parent home. We had no say in the schools we attended as kids. And we certainly had no choice in our socioeconomic status.

We were forced to grow up in the conditions unique to our family situation. I think this is an important distinction to make. How we were raised and what we were taught as children and young adults were mostly out of our control. Our upbringing, as well as our unique circumstances and social and familial conditioning, helped shape and mold us into who we have become today. Who is to blame for this? Our parents and caregivers? Teachers and society? And is "blame" even the right word? I am not sure. However, we do blame each other for our differences, and we do place bounties on each other's heads for factors we have no control over.

Of course, we can be responsible for how we choose to behave as adults, but what if you don't know any better? What if you never learned how to love the skin you're in, or how to not weaponize your skin color? Many of us didn't know any better until our anti-blackness was pointed out, or until we began our own journey of examining our internalized racism. The truth is we are all on journeys of personal liberation and evolution. What I know about my internalized anti-blackness today is strikingly different from what I knew five years ago. I am not the same person I was ten years ago. And although this truth doesn't minimize any anti-black harm I have caused, it would have been nice to have received more compassion (for being infected by whiteness) and grace (in the form of patience and understanding) from my fellow Black people.

Additionally, I would have liked to have had the knowledge to extend the same compassion and grace to Black folks who harmed me. I think we all deserve compassion and grace, and we all need to practice embodying it for other Black people who are not only different from us, but who are also in different stages of their evolutionary journeys. I believe this is love in action. Maya Angelou said it best: "Now that I know better, I do better."

Before I got educated about domestic violence by working at a domestic violence shelter in my early twenties and became a domestic violence and sexual assault advocate, I used to say harmful shit about women who chose to stay in abusive situations and relationships. For example, I might say, "If she is stupid enough to stay with him, then it is her fault if she keeps getting abused." I was ignorant and uninformed. Once I learned the truth about domestic violence, the cycle of violence, and its psychological effects on victims/survivors, I then knew better. I learned no matter what, the violence is never the victim/survivor's fault. I learned the fear and threats of violence are real. I learned that every four to seven seconds a person (almost always a woman) is abused in the United States. I learned leaving a violent relationship is the most dangerous time, because that is when the likelihood of homicide dramatically increases. I learned how to deeply empathize with women in these abusive relationships and to not blame them for being abused.

I did not know any of this until it was brought into my awareness and I was taught the truth about these situations. And ever since I have gained this insight and knowledge, I know better than to make harmful victim-blaming comments about victims/survivors. Before I knew better, I consciously and unconsciously caused harm to domestic violence survivors. I am grateful for the unearned grace in the process. Grace I am willing to extend to other Black folks who do not know any better.

When we refuse to see ourselves in each other's journeys, we become bitter and resentful. We "other" each other and devalue the differences among us. When we refuse to remember we too were once ignorant and uninformed, we become arrogant and unforgiving, and we withhold compassion. When we refuse to honor our differences, we put ourselves on pedestals. We become judge and jury over other Black people's perspectives and experiences. We become an unrelenting authority. And when we do all these things, we get frustrated with Black folks who are in different head spaces and different places in their journeys, and we become intolerant when they make decisions based on their unique spaces and places. We become unwilling to acknowledge who they are, and we fail to understand where they are at any given point in their evolutionary journey. And when we cannot, or refuse to, meet our fellow Black people where they are, we deem them problematic or antagonistic, and the bounty begins.

So, what does the bounty look like? Bounties can manifest as various forms of anti-black violence. It does not matter what kinds of bounties we place on each other's heads; they are all detrimental and deadly. Bounties can show up as defamation of character, public or private dragging, ostracizing from the community, incessant gossiping, public campaigns to silence voices, vengeful attempts to interfere with financial livelihoods, and cutting folks off from access to resources and opportunities.

Bounties have the same fundamental intentions as the Weapons of Whiteness, the Four D's: to deny, defend, derail, and destroy. The bounties we place on other Black folks seek to *deny* their inclusion, access, and humanity. The bounties we champion seek to *defend* our opinions and perspectives about other Black folks. The bounties we partake in seek to *derail* a Black person's success and achievement. The bounties we participate in seek to *destroy* a Black person's character, reputation, and bank accounts.

These bounties are acts of violence. It is the same violence white folks commit against us when we get out of line, fail to follow the rules, or act like "uppity negroes." Bounties do not serve to uplift each other; instead, they serve to incarcerate and tear each other down.

A few days before finalizing this chapter, a white woman sent me a video via email, saying it made her feel awkward and uncomfortable. I didn't know why she sent it, so I replied to her email and asked, "Why did you send this video to me, and who are you?" I did not get a response from her, so I decided to watch it. Essentially, it was a "bash Catrice" video in which a Black woman, who I'd had a disagreement with about feminism, said I was abusive and a lover of the patriarchy. When I first watched it, I must admit I was pissed. The video was full of lies and slander. Now mind you, our disagreement happened two years ago, and really wasn't anything significant. A disagreement I had chalked up to two different perspectives and nothing more. Apparently, she has been seething about it ever since. At the time, I had chosen to not trash or drag her, but to release her with love. In other words, I chose to move on, take no shit, and do no harm. I really thought she would be over it by now, as it was extremely trivial. However, I see she still has a bounty on my head. While watching the video, I was able to observe her Weapons of Whiteness playing out and the Four D's were on display. As I write this, she is in full-blown bounty hunter mode.

CHAPTER SEVEN | BOUNTY HUNTERS

Her internalized racism and anti-blackness is raging like wildfire. Just because we disagree on what feminism is? Sad. I know there are always two sides to every story, but based on her commentary about me in the video, you'd swear I did something intentionally harmful to her. But nah, just a disagreement about what feminism means and my unapologetic stance that I am not a feminist, I am a womanist. That's it. From her perspective, she believes our differences make it worth her while to spew lies, slander my name, and try to defame my character. Sigh. Such wasted energy. I moved on, but clearly she has not.

But this is what is important to know. When I peel away the layers of her smear campaign, there lies the real issue: she is chasing the fool's gold and needs me to get out of the way so she can get it. And all I will say in response is, "No problem, I will gladly move to the side so you can pursue whiteness, which will never see you as fully human." We use the master's tools to hunt each other way too often and the desire for proximity to whiteness is a compulsion we must fight against every single day. It is infectious and intoxicating.

Part of me wanted to lash out. Part of me wanted to hold her accountable. Part of me felt compassion for her. The voice inside me that won said, "It ain't worth it. You know the truth; just keep moving forward, because the energy we put out comes back to us." That is the voice I listened to. I chose to not pick up Weapons of Whiteness to destroy a Black woman. I made the choice to release her, again, with love. Maybe a time will come when I will hold her accountable for the slander, but now is not that time. And even with this choice, I still live by the motto, "Take no shit and do no harm." Sometimes we have to be okay with not telling our side of the story. Sometimes we must choose compassion over bounties. We have to understand when it's the puppet master who is pulling the strings, so we can cut ourselves loose. This is just one way we can get and remain free.

We use our internalized racism and anti-blackness to harm one another, and I am not saying we should not hold each other accountable for that harm. Instead, I am advocating for and challenging you to learn alternative, more effective, and more compassionate ways of dealing with each other when harm is caused. We cannot dismantle the master's white house of terror by using the same treacherous tools and tactics it was built with. In fact, by using the master's tools, we strengthen and expand the terrorism. If we keep doing the master's work, we will complete the master's plan, and the plan is to marginalize, oppress, and annihilate Black bodies. The plan is to make blackness extinct, and we are pawns in the plan. We are being used to weaponize our own self-hatred manifested as anti-black violence to do the master's devious work. We have become bounty hunters for the beast that hunts us.

In fact, many of us are showing up like the Black bounty hunter in the movie *Harriet*. We are delusional to think whiteness will ever see us as equal and fully human when we co-conspire with white people to hunt our own. They laugh at us while we continue to destroy one another. Is it possible to hold each other accountable for how we harm each other without destroying one another? It absolutely is, and I will share how in the upcoming chapters. An even better question is, can we disagree or dislike each other without feeling the need to enact a public smear campaign or a low-key social media drag?

Whether it is a public defamation campaign or a passive-aggressive drag, the core of this type of response is pettiness, pain, and projection. With all the ways whiteness and its bounty hunters are attacking Black folks, who really has time for this? Black folks who target other Black folks with malicious intent and destructive action are misappropriating their pain and weaponizing their petty to be agents of white terrorism. You may not like this truth, but it does not decrease its accuracy.

And let me state this truth again: *you can hold other Black folks accountable for the harm they cause you, but you do not have to become a bounty hunter.* Let us not adhere to and perpetuate the same Slave Codes of whiteness. Let us reclaim the Black Codes and make them truly ours so they embody the "Take no shit and do no harm" philosophy with significant doses of accountability and love.

LAY DOWN YOUR WEAPONS

WHITE TERRORISM: When white folks use Weapons of Whiteness to assault, insult, invalidate, silence, harm, and oppress Black and Brown folks.

How are you assaulting, insulting, and invalidating other Black people to silence, harm, and oppress them?

_____

_____

_____

_____

WHITE CODES: When white folks use a set of conscious and unconscious rules, guidelines, standards, and expectations to try to control and deny the agency and sovereignty of Black folks.

What codes, standards, or rules are you using to control the agency and sovereignty of Black folks?

_____

_____

_____

_____

CHAPTER SEVEN | BOUNTY HUNTERS

WHITE CLIPBOARDING: When white folks are obsessed with controlling the agency of Black and Brown folks, and do so by micromanaging their time, agendas, whereabouts, and schedules.

Are there certain kinds of Black folks who you constantly nitpick and critique? Why?

_____

_____

_____

_____

WHITE TRIANGULATION: When white folks try to pit one Black or Brown person against another Black or Brown person.

How have you tried to pit one Black person against another, and what was your motive and/or goal? Why?

_____

_____

_____

_____

> WE CAN DISAGREE AND STILL LOVE EACH OTHER UNLESS YOUR DISAGREEMENT IS ROOTED IN MY OPPRESSION AND DENIAL OF MY HUMANITY AND RIGHT TO EXIST.
>
> — JAMES BALDWIN

CHAPTER
EIGHT

BLACK CODES

One of the most painful feelings is when skin folk ain't kinfolk.
Catrice M. Jackson

"Stop right there! Where do you think you're going? Show me your papers, Gal! Show me your papers, Boy!"

That's the nice version of what white folks used to demand if they thought Black folks were in the wrong place. This is the shit white folks would say to Black folks who were minding their own damn business, just trying to survive in life. They would say it to enslaved Africans, and they would say it to the free Black folks who were no longer obligated to show their papers. This is one way white folks weaponized their whiteness to command agency over Black people's lives: by wielding the weapons of *White Entitlement* and *White Authority*. I defined these Weapons of Whiteness in Chapter 2, but as a reminder, *White Entitlement* is when white folks believe they have the right to think, do, say, and behave in whatever way they choose when engaging with Black folks, and they expect Black folks to answer their questions and comply with their requests and demands. Additionally, it's when white folks believe they can have what they want when they want it, and they expect to receive it.

White Authority is when white folks use their whiteness to dominate people, places, spaces, and things. When they think they can take up all the space, do all the talking, and have all the answers, that's White Authority too. Asking Black folks to show their papers are both these weapons in action, and this was common practice, especially when Black Codes were enacted.

At the end of the United States Civil War, white people replaced the original Slave Codes with Black Codes, which were rules and laws that criminalized and penalized Black people just for existing in Black bodies. Black Codes denied Black folks the opportunity to vote and to attend public schools, and in some states, they denied Black folks the right to equal treatment under the law. These discriminatory laws (which set the stage for Jim Crow laws) were passed in 1865, not coincidentally the same year the Thirteenth Amendment to the U.S. Constitution was passed. Section 1 of that amendment states, "Neither slavery nor involuntary servitude, except as a punishment for crime whereof the party shall have been duly convicted, shall exist within the United States, or any place subject to their jurisdiction."

In other words, if someone was convicted of a crime, they could be forced into involuntary servitude, which spawned the convict leasing system, aka "slavery by another name." And with the Black Codes in effect, white folks could arrest free Black folks for the crimes of being unemployed, roaming the streets, or "vagrancy" (which were purposefully vague laws that allowed authorities to arrest free Black people for no reason at all), and essentially force them back into slavery.

Free Black folks were not really free. Black Codes not only kept most Black folks dependent on their former owners, they also denied free Black people any sort of sovereignty. These codes degraded and dehumanized Black people, and they destroyed most opportunities for equality and equity. In other words, Black Codes allowed white people to continue to treat Black people like second-class citizens. Here we are in the 21st century, and not much has changed. Although the Black Codes are now officially illegal, white folks still have unwritten rules or Black Codes they believe Black folks should adhere to. Rules like not walking through a neighborhood with Skittles and iced tea, not being a twelve-year-old playing with a toy gun at a recreation center, and not barbequing in a public park. Black Codes also look like Black folks not being able to take a nap, sell water, sit in a Starbucks, swim in a pool, shop at a CVS, drive through a predominantly white neighborhood, or try to help an autism patient.

In each of these incidents, white folks discharged the weapons of White Entitlement and White Authority to police the whereabouts and behaviors of Black folks. White folks "called the police" on Black folks for engaging in normal, lawful activities. Why? Because white people have a deep-seated belief in their own entitlement and authority to determine when and how Black folks are out of place. White people still believe they have the right to control our bodies. This is the modern version of "Show me your papers, Boy or Gal!"

To this day, white folks are demanding that Black folks show their papers anywhere, any time, and any place to control Black people. We are still not free. And we participate in this continued captivity by acting as bounty hunters, enacting our own Black Codes, and requiring our fellow Black people to show us their papers. How have you used this weapon of anti-blackness, aka "show me your papers," with fellow Black folks? Have you ever questioned another Black person's ethnicity or identity based on skin tone or language? Have you ever challenged another Black person for showing up in places or spaces you deemed appropriate for only "certain kinds" of Black folks? Have you ever checked for another Black person's "Black card" to qualify them as being Black enough? I have done all three without realizing the harm I may have caused or the anti-blackness weapons I was using against my own people.

This is interesting, because white people do not really care about all our unique identities, nuances, and ethnicities beyond having Black skin. If you are Black, that's all they care about. They do not care if you are Nigerian, Haitian, Afro-Latina, or multiracial. They lump us all into the category of "Black" and treat us as such. But we know owning our identities matters, and the alternative is to lose big pieces of our soul, our heritage, our roots, and our culture.

I recently did the African American Ancestry DNA test and discovered my dominant African DNA is Cameroonian. This test is for Black folks, is based on research by Black folks, and is conducted by Black folks to make sure it is as accurate as possible. It is a matrilineal test, which means it specifically examines the DNA of your maternal ancestors. I especially appreciate this test because it also helps pinpoint which African tribes you come from. My tribes are the Tikar, Mafa, and Kotoko peoples of Cameroon. I am so thrilled to know this information about my ancestral roots and humbled to be a descendant of Cameroonian peoples. Since finding out more about my African roots, my sense of belonging has increased dramatically. Finally, I know where my ancestors originated from, and I am proud to be African. And even with all this pride, white folks will still see me as "just Black" and treat me like a second-class citizen. Knowing, honoring, and celebrating your heritage is beautiful, but it is important to emphasize that Black people often use this distinction as a Weapon of Whiteness against other Black people.

A few months back, I recall a Black woman talking about her Spanish ancestry and celebrating it, as she should. She was immensely proud of this part of her heritage, but then went on to say she was "Black" Black and not "mixed" Black. Huh? What is the difference? Is it better to be Black and Spanish versus being Black and white? I was confused. I was not sure exactly how to interpret what she was saying, but I presumed she was insinuating that Black people with European/white in their genes are not really Black people, while Black folks with Spanish in their genes are. From my understanding, I believe many Spanish people would consider themselves to be European, aka "white." I would draw the same conclusion. I did not ask her to clarify what she meant, but I wonder: does it really matter? Does it make a significant difference whether someone is Black and Spanish or Black and white? And if so, to what degree? And who gets to decide who is Black and who isn't? Is there a rule book to make these determinations?

Many Black folks feel the need to be the gatekeepers of blackness, meaning they love to size up other Black folks and determine whether they are Black enough to be allowed into Black spaces and Black gatherings. They love using the weapon of "show me your papers" to get Black folks or those who identify as Black to prove their blackness. To ask other Black folks to prove they are the "right amount of Black" before being accepted, allowed, or included. We do not trust each other to know who we are. We act as overseers of blackness, just like the master taught us to do. We are doing the master's oppressive work under the guise of "protecting" the community. In the case of the Rachel Dolezals of the world, however, this demand for papers is justified, because she is certainly a white woman who wants to be Black. But how do we know when someone is being a Rachel Dolezal? Boy, is that a fine and delicate line to walk, and I have caught myself walking it many times in my life. I do not have all the answers to knowing whether someone is pulling a Rachel Dolezal or not and what to do about it. But outside this type of "are you really Black" inquiry, I find it dehumanizing to gatekeep. Still, I see why it can be warranted in some cases.

I introduced Rachel Dolezal in Chapter 6. If you would like more details of who I'm talking about, just do a quick Google search of her name. In a nutshell, Rachel presented herself as a light-skinned, white-passing Black woman for years, and she was so convincing, she became the president of the NAACP chapter in Spokane, Washington. After she was outed for cultural appropriation and fraud in 2015, she resigned from that position. These days, Rachel Dolezal still self-identifies as Black and says she is transracial. Some folks argue that Rachel committed blackface by pretending to be Black, and I agree. And that is disrespectful and dehumanizing.

The potential harm to Black folks caused by this type of white terrorism and violent mockery is a good reason to gatekeep who is and isn't Black. Listen. I don't care how much makeup a white woman puts on or how texturized her hair is, her DNA is white, and within that DNA lie Weapons of Whiteness, and their purpose is to harm and destroy. In my opinion, the Rachel Dolezals of the world are the exception to the rule about not gatekeeping Black people's blackness. It is a divide-and-conquer tactic. And we cannot win with this strategy.

Have you ever acted as a gatekeeper of blackness by demanding to see another Black person's papers? I have. And although I do it less than I used to, it still happens. Unlearning how to weaponize the master's tools against Black people will be a lifelong journey for me and for you. With centuries of anti-black conditioning and indoctrination embedded into every fiber of society and our familial environments, it's going to take a lifetime to rid ourselves of this toxicity. Critiquing and analyzing the skin tone of our fellow Black folks is not the only way we command they show us their papers. Language, diction, vocabulary, and articulation are other ways we size up other Black folks to determine their degree of blackness so we can decide whether to allow them into our communities and cliques. And just about any Black person can require their criteria be met. I believe we all have conscious and unconscious criteria, or an invisible checklist, that we use to establish whether another Black person meets our definition of who is "Black enough" and/or who is "too Black."

We critique each other for being light-bright, Oreo, hotep, Blackity-Black, ghetto-fabulous, hood, ratchet, assimilated, ambiguous, Sambo, and every other "classification" we can think of to deny and destroy blackness. We critique each other for being formally educated, bourgeois, "articulate," conservative, radical, pro-black, uppity, and coons. Are these terms any less offensive than Mammy, Sapphire, or Jezebel, which were created and used primarily by white folks, meaning they are derogatory and anti-black in nature? Yet we frequently toss these words around to describe Black folks who are different from us to reinforce the restrictive Black Codes created by toxic whiteness. We use these terms as a way to command that other Black folks not only show their papers, but also pull their race card if deemed appropriate. If white folks stopped dehumanizing us and tearing us down, anti-blackness would still thrive, because we've allowed it to become a natural part of our rules of engagement with other Black folks.

This phenomenon reminds me of this quote by Lao Tzu: "If you give a hungry man a fish, you feed him for a day, but if you teach him how to fish, you feed him for a lifetime." Here's my restatement of this quote as it relates to anti-blackness: *"If you want to dehumanize a Black person, call them a derogatory name, but if you want to dehumanize generations of Black people, teach them how to hate themselves, and they will oppress their own people for generations."*

My rewording of Tzu's quote shows that the master's tools work as they were designed to, with sadistic efficiency. What purpose does it serve for you to call another Black person "Sambo," "coon," or "hotep"? Does it fatten your bank account? Does it expand your spirituality? Does it increase your social capital? I mean, what is the benefit for you? What value do you gain? How do these terms, phrases, and/or "show-me-your-papers" criteria make you a better person in mind, body, and soul? How do Black Codes advance the Black community, lift it up, or bring us closer to justice, equality, and liberation?

While I have been guilty of using Black Codes myself, each day I realize how they are not only dehumanizing, but also detrimental to the collective advancement of Black people. We love to shout, "We all we got," yet often, our head-hunting and intra-marginalization continue to divide, conquer, and derail our intention for Black liberation. There is a quote commonly attributed to Eleanor Roosevelt that says, "Small minds discuss people; average minds discuss events; great minds discuss ideas." This quote seems fitting for the questions I have raised here. The critique criteria, the invisible checklists, and the terms and phrases we use to describe other Black folks are small-minded.

They are small-minded, because is that the best we can do? Reduce our blackness down to name-calling, ridicule, and critique? They are small-minded, because although we have learned how to weaponize the color of our skin against each other, none of us chose this skin. They are small-minded, because we are so much more than dialect, skin tone, and hair texture. And in the grand scheme of things spiritually, we have far more worth than our appearance, and none of those characteristics or attributes make any of us better than the next Black person.

When I reflect on how everyone hates blackness, and on the pervasive, unrelenting anti-black attacks we face, these bounties we have out for one another are petty, grudging, and mean-spirited. And this small-mindedness sure as hell doesn't stop the white terrorism we all face on some level. We are not collectively gaining a thing by our own toxic anti-blackness;

instead, we are destroying what is magical, meaningful, and majestic about us as Black people.

Sometimes I sit back and think about how these bounties, Black Codes, and checklists are playing out all over the world, and what comes to mind is an enormous pus-filled wound that never healed and continues to ooze infection. There is a tremendous amount of pain, wounding, and trauma in the Black community. We are dying from a double-edged sword, because if white folks and NBPOC folks are not trying to kill us, we are killing ourselves. Every day.

As I have said many times already, I have participated in this wounding, and I regret it. But now my eyes are wide open, and I can't help but long for a different way of being and engaging for Black people. And although I have greater insight, it does not mean I'm free from these treacherous Weapons of Whiteness. It does mean, however, that I am significantly more conscious of them and work hard every day to not use them to destroy my fellow Black people. I may never master this in my lifetime, but I will spend the rest of my days knowing better, doing better, and being better. I believe you can do this too. And as a therapist, I believe refusing to be a bounty hunter, refusing to create and enact Black Codes, and refusing to determine another Black person's value by a set of criticizing criteria will begin to close the gaping wound and allow healing to begin and expand throughout the Black community.

To that end, you may not agree with what I am about to discuss next, yet I believe it is important to bring it into the equation for healing. I am also aware my perspective is one of a lighter-skinned Black person, and therefore, my intention is to say what comes next with caution and care. So, hear me out and read the rest of the book before you decide I don't know what I'm talking about, or that you're unwilling to consider the following points.

Yes, I know Black folks with darker skin, tighter coils, and more "African-looking" features experience greater discrimination and anti-blackness. I don't know how that feels personally, yet I believe every single person who says it happens to them, because I have used my hierarchical privileges to cause the same types of harm through bounties, Black Codes, and checklists. Reducing Black folks to appearance only and disregarding their worthiness is the master's work. It is violence.

Lighter-skinned people in particular have to acknowledge and own up to this intraracial violence and stop perpetrating it. We need to name it, claim it, and work hard every day to rid ourselves of these toxic tools of the master. This is our work to do. And it is not the responsibility of darker-skinned Black folks to teach us. We need to be proactive in putting down our anti-black Weapons of Whiteness daily.

Not too long ago, I was hosting an event for Black women at Harriet's Dream® (a racial trauma and healing center for Black women), where we were discussing the specific form of anti-blackness known as "light skin versus dark skin," and the harm this differentiation inflicts. There was an obvious elephant in the room, so I pointed it out by saying, "We lighter-skinned Black folks have caused deep harm to our darker-skinned sisters, and we need to own that shit." No one else wanted to address this, because it was more comfortable to dance around the issue of lighter-skinned Black folks causing harm. And most of the Black women in the room were of a lighter skin tone. Some of them looked shocked. Some tried to minimize the violence by declaring they have never caused that type of harm to darker-skinned Black women, and maybe one or two flat-out disagreed with my statement. I didn't allow for the lighter-skinned women to take up too much space; instead, I quickly opened up the discussion so the darker-skinned women could speak their truth.

I looked over at one of my darker-skinned sisters, and she had tears rolling down her face. I paused to allow her the space to feel and express her emotions, and then I asked her if there was anything she wanted to share. She said, "Catrice, I have never heard a light-skinned Black woman say what you just said. Most of the time they don't even know the harm they cause, or they deny it." And then she put her head down and continued to cry. She went on to share how she has been ridiculed, judged, and excluded by light-skinned Black people most of her life, especially when she was younger. I believed her. I affirmed her. And I apologized on behalf of lighter-skinned folks for the harm we cause her.

I thanked her for sharing, because she did not owe us an explanation. I encouraged her—to the extent she deems is appropriate for her—to continue to share her deep feelings about her real-life experiences with people she trusts. And I encouraged my sister to begin a personal healing journey to remove the daggers her own people have stabbed her with. I am hoping this was a powerful and pivotal moment not only for her, but for all the Black women in the room. I would have loved more time to process this moment and work through it with the women in attendance, but it will be an ongoing conversation at Harriet's Dream.

Talking about and working through the nuanced complexities of anti-blackness is necessary and triggering. Anti-blackness is a multidimensional monster that is relentless in its pursuit to devour Black bodies and Black joy. It's persistent and pervasive. And like white terrorism, it never sleeps. It is alive and thriving in every human body all over the world. We may not be able to do anything significant to stop it from hunting us, but we can stop hunting each other with it. To stop causing harm to one another, the approach for eradication and healing must be multidimensional as well. Although there is no one strategy, method, or technique that will kill the beast of anti-blackness that co-conspires with white terrorism to take us out, we can stop demanding to see each other's papers and using Black Codes.

As Black folks, each of us must actively participate in our own personal education and healing. And just as lighter-skinned Black folks need to stop weaponizing their skin color, darker-skinned folks must start working toward healing their wounds. And let me be clear about this truth: when lighter-skinned and white-passing Black folks lay down our weapons and commit to not using them, darker-skinned Black folks can catch their breath and begin to heal. We light-skinned folks are part of the problem. Lighter-skinned folks reading this... we got to stop this violent bullshit. Now.

What I'm talking about is no different from the expectation we have of white folks to stop their violence so we can catch our breath and begin to heal. Black folks are in a perpetual state of wounding. Wounding from white folks, NBPOC, and Black folks. It's astonishing to see Black folks endure in spite of the terrorism and violence we encounter on a daily basis. It's remarkable, and it speaks to both the burden and the badge of honor in being Black. But just imagine who we can become and what we can accomplish together if we lay down our weapons of destruction and division, and instead arm ourselves with tools of healing, unity, and collaboration. We've got a lot of undoing and unlearning to do.

We have been conditioned to give white folks the benefit of the doubt. To forgive them and offer them grace for their transgressions. But when are we going to offer the same grace to our fellow Black folks? This may be controversial, and you may not agree with it, but there is work to be done by all of us. Regardless of how we identify or what we look like, we must find a way to start our healing and evolutionary journeys to meet in the middle for reconciliation and unity. Otherwise, the master's house will never be dismantled, and we will continue to kill each other with his Weapons of Whiteness.

LAY DOWN YOUR WEAPONS

WHITE COLLUSION: When white folks willingly or unknowingly co-conspire with white terrorism and racism at the expense of Black and Brown folks. Also, when white folks choose white comfort over justice and equity for nonwhite people.

How have you sided with whiteness to put bounties on Black people?

_____
_____
_____
_____

Have you ever colluded with whiteness to defame or destroy another Black person? Why?

_____
_____
_____
_____

How does your White Collusion show up?

_____
_____
_____
_____

CHAPTER EIGHT | BLACK CODES

In what ways are you currently coddling whiteness and keeping it comfortable?

_____

_____

_____

_____

> YOU KNOW, IT'S NOT THE WORLD THAT WAS MY OPPRESSOR, BECAUSE WHAT THE WORLD DOES TO YOU, IF THE WORLD DOES IT TO YOU LONG ENOUGH AND EFFECTIVELY ENOUGH, YOU BEGIN TO DO TO YOURSELF.
>
> — JAMES BALDWIN

CHAPTER
NINE

TIME TO GET FREE AND HEAL

> You can't heal and get free when you hurt and oppress other black folks.
>
> Catrice M. Jackson

No one is responsible for your healing but you. Plenty of folks can be responsible for your trauma, but no one except you can do your critical healing work. You cannot afford to put this valuable act of freedom and love in anyone else's hands but your own. I believe all Black folks are wounded warriors in some phase of recovery from trauma. We have all been repeatedly wounded by white terrorism and anti-blackness over our lifetimes, with no real breaks to heal from the brutality and restore our divine sovereignty.

It's like we are swimming in this massive, infectious wound that is oozing nonstop with grief, sadness, violence, and rage. And every time we try to climb out of the wound to catch our breath and try to heal, another assault against the collective Black body is committed, and we are sucked back into the grief, sadness, violence, and rage. This wound is like a boil on the ass of America. Virulent. Infectious. Toxic and deadly. The boil of hatred, violence, oppression, and inhumanity has been on America's ass since day one, throbbing with terrorism, and every year it expands. Its pus is putrid and viscous, and the boil vehemently traps Black folks inside for centuries. We are a people in a perpetual state of survival. It's time for us to get free and thrive.

We did not enter the world wounded, per se, but we are highly predisposed to embodying a trauma response. I introduced Dr. Joy DeGruy in Chapter 4; whenever the subject of Black Americans and our generational trauma comes up, I consider her research and findings. She coined the phrase "Post Traumatic Slave Syndrome (PTSS)," which she defines as "...a set of behaviors, beliefs, and actions associated with, or related to, multigenerational trauma experienced by African Americans that include, but are not limited to, undiagnosed and untreated Post Traumatic Stress Disorder (PTSD) in enslaved Africans and their descendants."

Dr. DeGruy further suggests that due to centuries of enslavement, Jim Crow laws, and the ongoing, pervasive, systemic, and systematic racism and oppression in the United States, the Black community (especially descendants of enslaved Africans) has consciously and unconsciously developed multigenerational maladaptive behaviors. And these maladaptive behaviors are passed down from Black parents to Black children as survival strategies that embody the dichotomy of living in Black skin: we are in a constant cycle of survival and violence as we try to defend ourselves from white terrorism, and we are simultaneously harming one another with a different shade of lethal white terrorism. Since our arrival here in these violent states of America, we have been forced into this cycle of survival and violence, and we have become so accustomed to it we often don't realize we are part of the storm.

Another important point Dr. DeGruy makes is "...the syndrome continues because the children of parents indoctrinated into PTSS inadvertently become indoctrinated with the same behaviors, long after the behaviors have lost their contextual effectiveness." In other words, some of the behaviors adopted by enslaved Africans served them well during their desperate need to survive, but the anti-black strategies they used and passed down to us now work to our detriment. You may be thinking you need anti-black behaviors and checklists to survive, but you don't. Not within the Black community. Not when we each do our own personal healing. Not when we refuse to use Weapons of Whiteness against each other.

Imagine if I had a magic wand, and I could erase the cellular and mental memories of the past generations of anti-blackness. Imagine if I could make every Black person who is alive today forget what anti-black Weapons of Whiteness are. Imagine if we had the power to see each other with only loving, compassionate, and forgiving eyes. Imagine if there were no bounty hunters, Black Codes, checklists, or critique criteria to use as weapons against each other. How would we see each other? How would we treat each other? How would we feel? And what would the state of blackness look like around the world? PTSS continues to exist because we continue to perpetuate it. We have cut ourselves loose from a few of the master's puppet strings, but there are so many we're still attached to, and we're still dancing to his tune.

See. The more we cling to our internalized anti-blackness, the less we love, heal, and thrive. Many of us talk about breaking generational curses, but have you considered that internalized anti-blackness is one of the biggest curses with the greatest stranglehold on Black lives? Imagine the state of Black lives if we collectively worked on breaking just this one generational curse. The one that commands us to hate ourselves. The one that causes us to put bounties on blackness. The one that critiques instead of celebrates. We may never be able to slay the beast of white terrorism that hunts us, but we can stop feeding it with anti-blackness, for it thrives off our own treachery against one another. When we break this one generational curse, I believe we can meet in the middle for reconciliation and unity. On the way to the middle, we must each walk our individual path on this healing journey. On that long walk, each of us must commit to allowing the fragmented pieces of our wounding to fall from our being like leaves falling from a tree.

Undoing and unlearning generations of maladaptive thoughts, beliefs, and behaviors is going to take a lot of work, and it will not be easy. And while therapy may help, there is no "scientific" treatment for undoing this curse. We must work as a collective to orchestrate and sustain this type of healing social change for us, and we must continue to fight against systemic racism and white terrorism. We must still wage these two battles. And the battle to end anti-black violence among ourselves is a noble and necessary one. United we thrive. Divided we barely survive.

Healing. It's a verb. A daily, moment-by-moment, breath-by-breath, intentional, and conscious decision to take action. Before we take a deep dive into various healing strategies for freedom and liberation in the next chapter, it's important to share different versions of what personal healing can look like for you. Your healing does not and should not look like anyone else's, and there are numerous ways to heal. If you search the Internet, you will find several definitions for the word "healing." Some include outcomes, like "to be healthy again," "to be sound or whole," "to restore health," "to be free from ailment," "to bring to an end," and "to settle or reconcile." I believe all these outcomes are possible, depending on your circumstances. However, some of them, like "healthy again" are particularly challenging, especially if you are not able to pinpoint or articulate what "healthy" means for you. For example, if your emotional abuse started when you were a four-year-old child, you probably can't remember what life was like for you before then. Thus, even if you have spent most of your life trying to heal, you probably do not know or remember what healthy feels like. You may be unsure of what your preexisting condition of normalcy was like, or what it means to be "sound or whole."

There are too many variables to come up with a definition of "healing" that resonates for everyone, so I suggest you create your own. Personally, I like the phrase *"to be free from ailment,"* because although most folks may not know what they want, they often know what they do not want. And most people do not want an ailment, which can be an illness, sickness, disease, disorder, or condition. Who wouldn't want to be free from those?

I think this phrase is perfect for Black folks who have literally been captive in more ways than one, and because globally and collectively, we have been trying to *get free from* and *rid ourselves of* toxic whiteness and colonialism. We have been trying to get free from the illness, sickness, and dis-ease of whiteness. We have been trying to get free from PTSS, which is a disorder. We have been trying to get free from the conditions forced on us, including discrimination, social and environmental racism, and oppression. Since being forced into these United States, we have been trying to rid ourselves of all these things, with the end goal of being free and liberated from the system of white terrorism that ails us every day. Thus, this is the aspect of healing I choose to believe, tap into, and use for my own liberation. *To be free from ailment.* Maybe this definition feels right for you too.

So, what ails *you*? What conditions, illnesses, sicknesses, and diseases do you want to get free from? "Conditions" could mean circumstances, restrictions, environments, or requirements. Do you like the circumstances you are in? Do you have people or things restricting your joy and/or limiting your ability to thrive? Are you being slowly killed by your environment or by trying to anticipate and fulfill all the master's capricious requirements? There are many ways to define illness, sickness, and disease. What is infecting your mind, body, and spirit? What situations do you want to escape or get free from?

These are important questions I would like you to ask yourself and to explore. These are questions that open the door to deep healing and transformation. And taking action to heal begins the process of getting free from what ails you and keeps you captive. Taking consistent, intentional action to free yourself is what expands and sustains healing. I realize this is sometimes easier said than done. There are situations or conditions I need to free myself from that I have not yet been able to accomplish, because I have failed to take consistent, intentional action. And I know exactly why I have not done so. Maybe this rings true for you. Maybe you too know what is ailing you, but you have not started the healing process, either because you are procrastinating, you don't know what to do, or you simply refuse to take action.

I will use a personal situation to explain this further. Remember I said earlier in this chapter we sometimes do not remember what our preexisting condition of normalcy was? One of my healing issues is carrying extra weight. I think the last time in my life that weight was not an issue of some sort was in the third grade, when I was about eight or nine years old. And although we might remember bits and pieces of early childhood, not all those recollections are crystal clear. So, my memory of what "normal" weight feels like both physically and psychologically is fuzzy. Without this clear knowledge, how do I really know what normalcy is? How do I get back to something I do not remember? That's half my challenge, because I only know what life with extra pounds feels like. And although I do not have a major problem with how my body looks, I don't care for the way I feel in this body with extra weight, especially as I've gotten older.

What is the other half of my challenge? It is not an issue of self-esteem, because even though I'm carrying extra pounds or considered to be overweight, it hasn't affected my drive, ambition, or confidence in the pursuit of my goals and desires. And it isn't lack of knowledge—I know how to lose weight. I have lost large amounts of weight during my lifetime, including a recent fifty-pound loss as a prerequisite for knee surgery. The challenge for me is consistent, intentional action to eat healthy and exercise.

Why is the consistent, intentional action I need to engage in still a challenge? Because I have not made it an unwavering priority; instead, I have made my career and family my priorities. This is where my healing needs to begin. This is the work I need to do. This is the work I am doing now. Earlier I asked, "What ails you?" I ask myself that same question all the time: "What condition do I want to get free from?" My answer is the on-again, off-again cycle of prioritizing my health. This is where my freedom and liberation lie. Healing requires excavation; it requires a deep dive into your soul to mine for not only the answers, but also the magic you have hidden or forgotten. I firmly believe *we know the answers we seek, and our souls know the way.* So, like you, I am going to have to excavate into my soul to find the answer to the question, "What is stopping me from making my physical health my unwavering, number one priority?" Then I will have to take consistent, intentional action to set myself free from my ailment. Only I can do my healing work. What excavations do you need to do? What magic is forgotten or hidden that you need to rediscover to activate your own healing? This is your work. This is how you get free. It's how we all get free. Healing is not intellectual; it's transactional. Do your work.

They are trying to kill us. They want us sick, paralyzed, diseased, and dead. White terrorism is lurking in every space and place. The beast is hunting us. It lurks in the hospitals, schools, grocery stores, courthouses, college campuses, and doctors' offices. It lurks at the beaches, in the parks, in neighborhoods, and in every public place. While you are sleeping, it is lurking. It is hard to heal when you are being hunted. It is hard to heal when there is no safe place for black bodies, sometimes not even in your own home.

The relentless and continuous bounty whiteness puts on our heads can make us hypervigilant, suspicious, and uneasy, which means we can be in a constant state of anxiety. Anxiety can show up as nervousness, worry, phobias, upset stomach, irritable bowel syndrome (IBS), and generalized fear. You may also have symptoms like nausea, headaches, insomnia, fatigue, increased heart rate, rapid breathing, sweating, shortness of breath, trembling, and/or muscle tension or pain. Black folks may have all these symptoms, but we may also experience feelings of always being on guard, ready to defend ourselves, being extra sensitive, fearing something will go down at any moment, and/or being keenly aware of our surroundings. These behaviors are part of what we know as generational wisdom; they are survival skills. However, they are not only anxiety-producing behaviors, they are also symptoms of anxiety.

Unfortunately, symptoms of anxiety, along with the real experiences unique to Black folks, sound a lot like post-traumatic stress disorder (PTSD). And if you have been a victim of racially motivated insults, assaults, and invalidations repeatedly over your lifetime, you've experienced trauma. These symptoms of anxiety and repeated racial trauma can turn into other full-blown mental health disorders, such as generalized anxiety disorder (GAD), panic disorders, social anxiety, phobias, depression, and/or obsessive-compulsive disorder (OCD). But note that these official diagnoses, listed in the *Diagnostic and Statistical Manual of Mental Disorders,*

Fifth Edition (DSM-5), could also be clusters of symptoms caused by living in the U.S. with Black skin. For example:

- *Being Black causes generalized anxiety (GAD)*
- *When you feel hunted, you will panic (panic disorders)*
- *It is not uncommon to have anxiety in social settings, especially if they are predominantly white settings (social anxiety)*
- *Racial fear, whether conscious or unconscious, is real and persistent (phobias)*
- *Racial anxiety can be depressing (depression)*
- *It's easy to be obsessed with protecting yourself from racism and white violence (OCD)*

As you know, merely trying to survive in Black skin is a perceived threat to the beast that hunts us. And while we try to survive, our physical and mental health are compromised, and symptoms are exacerbated.

Surviving while Black increases our risk for physical health problems such as asthma, migraines, vision problems, and back problems. Persistent and prolonged racial stress can manifest as ulcers and other gastrointestinal problems, as well as high blood pressure, heart disease, and stroke. No wonder high blood pressure (aka hypertension) is highest among African Americans, with an estimated forty percent of Black folks in this country diagnosed with it. White folks write this epidemic off, saying it's because we are allegedly more sensitive to salt and more likely to be obese, but they'll never tell the full truth: Black folks live in a constant state of fear and anxiety due to white terrorism, which increases cardiovascular stress. Our fear and anxiety is justified, due to the historical and current violence against Black bodies. Our fear and anxiety is real, and it's killing us. Because there has never been a time when Black bodies in this country were not being used, abused, commodified, and killed.

Healing is possible, but systematic and systemic racism make it difficult. If you go to the doctor or hospital, you know you are likely to not be believed, to have your pain minimized, to have your symptoms ignored, and to be treated discriminatorily. I am not discouraging you from going to the doctor or hospital. I am instead encouraging you to find Black clinicians and health professionals to provide medical services to you and your family. I am encouraging you to know your rights, and to strongly advocate on your own behalf and on behalf of your loved ones. I'm encouraging you to prioritize your physical and mental health as much as you can. I am encouraging you to move your body and eat the healthiest food you can access. I'm encouraging you to drink water and stay hydrated. I am encouraging you to sleep and rest as much as you can. I am encouraging you to pray and meditate. I am highly encouraging you to go back to your ancestral roots for wisdom on how to cure or minimize any physical ailments you have.

And if you choose to see a mental health professional, I'm encouraging you to find someone who matches your identity in as many ways as possible, so they have some idea of what you are dealing with. Most importantly, I am strongly encouraging you to examine how you too are infected with

CHAPTER NINE | TIME TO GET FREE AND HEAL

toxic whiteness, and to begin detoxing yourself to remove anti-blackness from your mind, body, and spirit. This is how we get free.

With literal, legal, environmental, and medical bounties on our Black heads, why would we want to put bounties out on each other? Because the beast of white terrorism not only wants us to be sick with physical ailments and diseases, it also wants us to be sick with toxic whiteness. And it wants us to infect each other so we emotionally die. If you have a headache, your whole body is affected by the pain and discomfort. When one of us hurts, we all hurt. We need individual healing, and we need collective healing. The whole body of blackness. The infection of whiteness contaminates our agape (aka divine) love for one another. It contaminates our thoughts and perceptions of one another. We become suspicious and judgmental of one another. We critique, criticize, and condemn one another.

Some of us have ingested so much pus from the wound we're all swimming in that we've become the pus, and we work against those who are trying to escape the boil on America's ass by pulling them back into the infectious cesspool of violence and self-hatred. If you are currently feeling bitter and angry with Black folks, seething with rage about what Black folks have done to you, and/or plotting to destroy another Black person, you've ingested so much pus it's eating you alive. You are doing the master's work and hunting your own people. You are becoming the infection and emotionally dying from it.

I know Black people have harmed you. They have talked about you and tarnished your name. Physically assaulted you. Ignored and excluded you. I know you've been betrayed and belittled by Black people. They have come for you, and maybe they have even dragged you for filth. I know Black people have abandoned you and called you out your name. They have silenced you. I know Black people have ridiculed you and mocked your blackness. They have chosen whiteness over you and betrayed your trust.

There is no denying all this is true, and you have experienced more than I can express in one chapter. I believe you. I am sorry it's happened, and if I've harmed you in any way, I'm sorry for that too. As I asked in Chapter 7, is it possible to hold each other accountable without destroying one another? It is our birthright to hold other Black people accountable. I believe we can, and we should. This is OUR work. This is one path to our freedom and liberation.

LAY DOWN YOUR WEAPONS

WHITE FALSE PRIDE: When white folks believe they are exceptional, distance themselves from white terrorism, and self-proclaim their Allyship.

How does your exceptionalism show up? How are you distancing yourself from the pain and plight of other Black people?

_____

_____

_____

_____

WHITE POSITIVITY: When white folks weaponize positivity to minimize and excuse racial assaults and/or use spiritual bypassing to deflect and deny racist acts.

How do you use the weapon of positivity to minimize Black people's lived racial experiences? How do you use spirituality or religion to avoid the discomfort of talking about racism?

_____

_____

_____

_____

WHITE INTELLECTUALIZING: When white folks fail to express empathy for the racism Black and Brown folks experience, and instead respond from a cognitive and intellectual space.

In what ways have you detached from your own pain that's been caused by (or is related to) white terrorism and anti-blackness?

_____

_____

_____

_____

Are there certain "kinds" of Black folks you do not empathize with? Why?

_____

_____

_____

_____

DO I REALLY WANT TO BE INTEGRATED INTO A BURNING HOUSE?

JAMES BALDWIN

CHAPTER
TEN

SEPARATION FOR LIBERATION

> We don't have to be in relationship with each other
> to love one another and be in community.
>
> Catrice M. Jackson

Every single Weapon of Whiteness white folks use against us is a weapon we use against each other. But we call the weapons hate, shade, smoke, and heat, and like fire they burn, harm, engulf, and destroy. Sometimes we call them "accountability and dragging," while other times we call them "coming for someone." It does not matter what you call these menacing master's tools, when they are used by Black folks against Black folks, they are weapons of interpersonal violence and anti-blackness. And they are used with the same intentions as when white folks use them, the Four D's: to deny, defend, derail, and destroy. Throughout this book, I have discussed several reasons why I believe we continue to use these weapons against each other. In this chapter, I will discuss two more: trauma bonding and internalized oppression, and I will also discuss healing strategies for freedom and liberation.

Trauma, be it physical or psychological, tends to elicit classic trauma responses such as fear, anxiety, defensiveness, hypervigilance, and grief. It's natural to be so afraid and

CHAPTER TEN | SEPARATION FOR LIBERATION

nervous that you simultaneously attack and protect. You may find yourself as both a recipient and a perpetrator of the cycle of violence I described in Chapter 3. This cycle can be experienced in intimate relationships, friendships, and casual relationships. It certainly does not discriminate.

White folks inflict violence on us, and we inflict violence on each other. How is that working out for us? We are in a perpetual cycle of violence; understanding this truth is one way we can begin to escape the trauma bond with white terrorism to heal our trauma wounds. Let's start with the *trauma bond*. There are several definitions and schools of thought about what trauma bonding is. It has been described as a unique form of manipulation characterized by repetitive behaviors committed by narcissistic people to keep the cycle of violence going, resulting in a traumatic bond every time an abusive act is committed. Another definition is when a person remains loyal and in relationship with someone who is physically, emotionally, and/or psychologically destructive (aka a narcissist). And finally, trauma bonding can be described as an abusive relationship with a narcissist, where dehumanizing, devaluing, and discarding is a repetitive cycle. You may have noticed the word "narcissism" as a common component in these three definitions. Narcissists are some of the most treacherous and debilitating people to be in relationship with. And we Black people are indeed in a violent and narcissistic relationship with toxic whiteness.

Simply put, and as I defined it in Chapter 3, narcissism is a combination of personality traits and behaviors that are manipulative, controlling, and abusive. A grandiose sense of entitlement is a key characteristic, along with arrogance, exploitative tendencies, envy obsession, and a lack of empathy for others. Narcissists crave and need admiration. They are extremely preoccupied with power and dominance, and they believe they are exceptional and unique. But a narcissist's primary trait is they gaslight the hell out of people. White folks, white terrorism, and whiteness are narcissistic, and thus they too are manipulative, controlling, and abusive in their relationships with us. This has been true since our first contact with them, and centuries later, nothing has changed.

Yet we continue to be in relationship with white folks even though we know they are narcissists. This is our trauma bond with whiteness, as evidenced by the fact that our relationship with white folks (and with whiteness itself) involves them dehumanizing us, devaluing us, and—when we don't perform their idealized version of blackness or be their "magical negro" (a Black person who appeases their every desire and command)—discarding us. Our relationship with whiteness is physically, emotionally, and/or psychologically destructive as we spin continuously in its cycle of violence. We hope and pray. We chant and march. We resist and persist. We protest and fight, yet whiteness repeats the cycle of violence, decade after decade, manipulating us into staying in relationship with it, both collectively and as individuals. This is a trauma bond, a multigenerational trauma bond. And in my opinion, it's a generational curse.

Over five decades ago, Dr. Martin Luther King Jr. said, "I fear I am integrating my people into a burning house," and we are still engulfed in violent flames. I believe Dr. King saw evil in the flammable storm. A storm he was leading his people, Black people, into with his quest for equality and integration. Toward the end of his life, I suspect Dr. King realized that peaceful protests and civil disobedience were not going to get Black folks to the promised land, nor his dream fulfilled. I believe Dr. King looked the beast (white terrorism) in the eye many times and was horrified by the malevolence and callousness he saw there. Generations of Black people before Dr. King experienced this violent White Gaze; after staring at it daily, he understood the eye was not going to blink, let alone change. And although there have been significant advances in civil rights and social change has occurred, the White Gaze, the malevolent eye of whiteness, is still indifferent, cold-hearted, and often lethal. The cycle of violence viciously spins with no intention of slowing down or stopping, and we help spin that thing like we are trying to win a chance at the showcase on *The Price Is Right*. We may not be able to stop this game show from playing, but we sure as hell do not have to sit in the audience, run up on stage, and spin that damn wheel.

Brother Malcolm, on the other hand, believed in separation, not integration. Although he slightly relaxed his stance about integration shortly before his assassination, he was all for stepping out of the cycle of violence, breaking trauma bonds with the beast, and separating ourselves from toxic whiteness. He had no qualms about his perspective on what "negroes" should do to free themselves from the beast's grip to live liberated and free, and he shared them in a 1963 interview at the University of California, Berkeley. Here is quote from that interview:

> Our people in the Negro community are trapped in a vicious cycle of ignorance, poverty, disease, sickness, and death. There seems to be no way out. No way of escape.

The wealthy educated Black bourgeoisie, those uppity Negroes who do escape, never reach back and pull the rest of our people out with them. The Black masses remain trapped in the slums.

And because there seems to be no hope or no other escape, we turn to wine, we turn to whiskey, and we turn to reefers, marijuana, and even to the dreadful needle—heroin, morphine, cocaine, opium—seeking an escape.

Many of us turn to crime, stealing, gambling, prostitution. And some of us are used by the white over lords downtown to push dope in the Negro community among our own people. Unemployment and poverty have forced many of our people into a life of crime. But the real criminal is in the City Hall downtown, in the State House, and in the White House in Washington, D.C. The real criminal is the white liberal, the political hypocrite. And it is these legal crooks who pose as our friends, force us into a life of crime, and then use us to spread the white man's evil vices in our community among our own people.

The Honorable Elijah Muhammad teaches us that our people are scientifically maneuvered by the white man into a life of poverty. Because we are forced to live in the poorest sections of the city, we attend inferior schools. We have inferior teachers and we get an inferior education. The white power structure downtown makes certain that by the time our people do graduate, we won't be equipped or qualified for anything but the dirtiest, heaviest, poorest-paying jobs. Jobs that no one else wants.

CHAPTER TEN | SEPARATION FOR LIBERATION

We are trapped in a vicious cycle of economic, intellectual, social, and political death. Inferior jobs, inferior housing, inferior education which in turn again leads to inferior jobs. We spend a lifetime in this vicious circle. Or in this vicious cycle going in circles. Giving birth to children who see no hope or future but to follow in our miserable footsteps.

—Malcolm X at University of California, Berkeley, October 11, 1963

Whoa! Brother Malcolm's truths are still relevant today. Black folks are still suffering from "poverty, disease, sickness, and death." Collectively, we are still "trapped in a vicious cycle of economic, intellectual, social, and political death." And for many of us, there is still "no way out. No way of escape...no hope." I sometimes wonder where we would be as a people if more of our elders and ancestors had followed Malcolm X's teachings. Would they have been able to follow his commandments? Could they have built Black communities and taken care of their own? A better question is, can the Black folks of today accomplish Brother Malcolm's vision? Do we now have the capacity to build our own communities and take care of our own people, Black people? Do you think we Black people even want this reality or society for ourselves, or are we so entrenched in the trauma bond with whiteness that we believe we cannot survive and thrive without white folks?

Not a whole lot has changed for Black folks since Malcolm's speech in 1963, so I draw several conclusions: we suffer from a severe case of collective PTSS, we are plagued by white terrorism, and we don't know how to effectively break our trauma bonds with whiteness. As with anything you wish to change, you must first identify and name it. What would you call the Black collective's inability to break free? A dis-ease? An addiction? Codependency? Whatever you call it, it is real, but it is also something we can rid ourselves from and overcome. I realize Black folks are at different stages of their journey to freedom: some have not broken free at all, some are only partially free, and some are trying to complete their journey.

Which one is true for you? I am partially free. As I described in Chapter 2, my deep dive into Black freedom and liberation started in 2012 when Trayvon Martin was murdered. My heart was broken into a million pieces, and for the first time, violence against Black bodies became personal to me. Yup, it had to hit home for it to hit deep. At the time, my son was almost twenty years old, and all I could think was, "It could have been my son." Since then, I have been waking up more each day to the realities of white terrorism and anti-blackness. And in 2015, I finally walked away from my marketing and branding work to answer the call to be a voice and freedom fighter for racial justice. Every day I work toward separation and getting free.

I have often asked other Black people what freedom means for them. What does freedom sound like? Feel like? If you could wake up in the morning and be completely free, who would you be? How would you speak? How would you move through the world? What would you do, and what kind of life would you live? I have asked myself the same questions repeatedly over the past five years. And more specifically, I have also thought about what it means to live free and die trying. I will start with what I mean by "freedom." If I were truly free

CHAPTER TEN | SEPARATION FOR LIBERATION

in America, I would never have to experience the *White Gaze*, which is a Weapon of Whiteness I define as when white folks stare at Black people with violent curiosity and disdain, and when they snoop into Black spaces to consume Black thought and Black culture.

Man... can you imagine just moving through the world without white folks staring you up and down, being all up in your business, and questioning your mere existence? If there was no such thing as the violent White Gaze, almost half the white terrorism we experience would be eliminated. I believe most acts of white terrorism begin with the White Gaze. They gaze. They call the police. They gaze. They steal our culture. They gaze. They murder us. They gaze. They fetishize us. They gaze. They invade our space and violate our bodies. They gaze. They touch our children. They gaze. Intrusive. Predatory. Violent. If white folks would stop gazing, I could be completely free. Everywhere I go, white folks gaze at me.

Although I am mostly unbothered by the gaze, I know what it can do. I know its potential danger. I know what happens when white folks expect you to respond to their gaze and you refuse. I know the gaze is always upon me, and under the right circumstances, it can kill me. If I were completely free, I would not have to demand equality and equity. If I were completely free, I would not have to demand to be treated with dignity, respect, and care wherever I went. My pain would be real. My anger would be justified. If I were completely free, my family would be completely free. I would not have to be in constant prayer for my Black husband, son, and grandchildren. If I were completely free, I wouldn't have to take security precautions while I do my work. I wouldn't have to have a plan for when

I get stopped by the police. I could write an entire book about all the ways being completely free would feel like for me. How about you? What does freedom look and feel like for you? Is freedom obtainable for you? And specifically, how is the White Gaze keeping your freedom captive?

White folks do not have to worry about the Black gaze. In fact, the opposite is true for them: when Black people gaze, stare, or look on with curiosity at white people, it is immediately considered threatening and intimidating. Our Black gaze can get us fired, written up, attacked, or murdered. This is not freedom. The White Gaze holds us in perpetual captivity. It is the catalyst for many other forms of white terrorism we experience. But even though we can't escape the White Gaze, we cannot stop fighting for our freedom. We must live as free as we can and die trying, because as Angela Davis says, "Freedom is a constant struggle."

I recently watched a video in which Nebraska State Senator Ernie Chambers talked about how he has spent his whole adult life fighting for freedom, especially for Black folks. And how at age eighty-two, he is still fighting, but not yet free. One of the key things he said is our freedom lies in our power to vote, and voting can change things for Black people. He plans to continue fighting for Black people's freedom until he takes his last breath. I share his sentiments. Like Senator Chambers, I don't think we will have complete freedom in my lifetime, but it is my duty to fight for it until I take my last breath, so future generations may eventually gain it. In the meantime, I will do what is necessary, by any means necessary, to be free—and I will die trying.

CHAPTER TEN | SEPARATION FOR LIBERATION

When I say "die trying," I mean speaking up about racial injustice, staring white terrorism in the face to defy it, teaching white folks to lay down their Weapons of Whiteness, offering opportunities for Black folks to be empowered and healed, and centering and prioritizing Black lives. I will march, protest, rally, and shut white terrorism down. And one of my most important actions will be to educate my children and grandchildren about white terrorism and Black power. I will prepare them to carry the torch until either freedom comes or Black people take it. At this point, it ain't coming any time soon, so we must demand and take our freedom individually and collectively.

The first step is to lay down the Weapons of Whiteness we use against each other, for collective unity and collective victory. We will never get our freedom if we give energy to harming and destroying one another, and toxic whiteness knows this and is banking on it. Our trauma bond is so entrenched that we must take every action big and small to break free. You must find your own ways to release the chokehold the trauma bond has on your life, or we'll be saying "I can't breathe" for centuries to come. We have to snatch the horrendous hands of white terrorism from the neck of the Black collective, because it is relentless in its desire to strangle the life out of us. What will you do to separate from the toxic relationship you're in with whiteness? What will you do to liberate yourself and the Black collective?

I have the rare opportunity to work for myself, to be my own boss, and to work from home, so my contact with white folks is selective and limited. I realize not everyone wants to or can do this, but I have to say, the reduced contact is great for my mental health and mortality, and it will hopefully increase my longevity. One of the tenets I teach white folks is, "Wherever there are white people, there is racism. And the more white folks in a space, the more racism Black people experience." Racism is deadly. It smothers, hinders, oppresses, marginalizes, and kills. I believe Brother Malcolm was right: the more you can separate yourself from whiteness, the more the quality of your emotional life will improve. If the idea of separation resonates with you, work on it every day. Little by little, begin to break free from the grip and bondage of whiteness. You can do so in a variety of simple ways.

For example, several years ago, I removed artwork and home decor from my living space that didn't represent blackness and/or my African heritage, and I instead surrounded myself with beautiful pieces depicting people who look like me and my ancestors. This may seem trivial, but when I am in one of the safest places for me, it brings me peace. It comforts, empowers, and inspires. What I see in my living space reminds me of who I am and whose I am. I am a descendant of African Queens and Kings. I am a daughter of the most high King. I am reminded that blackness is beautiful, brilliant, and powerful. You may not be able to avoid whiteness completely, but you can make your living space reflect your celebration of blackness.

I have done something similar with my living room bookshelves. I got rid of ninety-five percent of the books written by white authors and others who uphold the worldview of whiteness, and replaced them with the works of Black authors, leaders, scholars, and influencers. I believe everything has energy, and I refuse to infuse my living space with objects of whiteness. I continue to purge whiteness from my internal and external spaces, and doing so intensifies my freedom. I feel more liberated.

What can you purge from your life, and what can you add to it, to be and feel more liberated? Actions I suggest are to define what the master's fool's gold (whiteness) looks like for you, how you chase it, and in what ways you can separate yourself and divest from it. How can you decrease the amount of White Gaze you experience? In what ways will you reinvest in your blackness and the blackness of other Black folks? I believe we have been led into the fire of toxic whiteness, and if you don't create and execute a plan to escape the blaze, you'll be saying "I can't breathe" for the rest of your life. It's time for intentional separation.

We are in a burning house, Folks! We cannot wait on the firefighters or the paramedics; we have to become them to save ourselves. In earlier chapters, I talked about the bounties, Black Codes, and other Weapons of Whiteness we use against each other. Imagine being inside a burning house full of Black people, and some of your fellow Black folks are preventing others from escaping. You see fellow Black people blocking the only exit. You see fellow Black folks pouring more gasoline on the fire. You see fellow Black people lying down and refusing to get up and run. You see fellow Black people boarding up the windows so no one can escape. No one is coming to save us, and we are keeping each other trapped inside this house of horrors that's been ablaze since 1619.

The Black collective is so intoxicated by whiteness, we cling to an engulfed house that is determined to incinerate us. By recognizing the fire, and by identifying how you're still clinging to the burning house, you can begin the process of separation for liberation. We have to escape the fire so we can begin our collective healing and restoration.

I believe intentional separation in all the ways possible for you is one action you can take, but that alone will not be enough to release the beast's grip or its trauma bond. I introduced the concept of chasing fool's gold in Chapter 5, and this is another factor for you to examine and respond to. Here are some questions for you to consider:

- *What does fool's gold look like for you? In what ways have you deemed whiteness and its manifestations as the norm, the gold standard, or the dream and aspiration?*
- *What is receiving your attention and life source because of whiteness' seductive lies?*
- *When you pull out your invisible checklist of exclusionary criteria for Black folks, what's on the list?*
- *What anti-black myths are you still believing and acting on?*

Your answers to these questions will help you understand how you pursue fool's gold, the imaginary promises and rewards whiteness says you will gain, receive, and/or have access to if you behave like a good negro by doing what whiteness does. Separating from and releasing the grip of the trauma bond require you to identify these lies and myths so you can free yourself from them. This is how the fire burns. It's the fuel for the storm. It is the food for the beast. And to truly understand your relationship with fool's gold, you must examine what

CHAPTER TEN | SEPARATION FOR LIBERATION

whiteness wants. Repeating the master's violence is not how we will get free. Here is a partial list of what whiteness wants:

- *Whiteness wants you to let its priorities dictate your focus.*
- *Whiteness wants to use you to do its dirty work.*
- *Whiteness wants you to use its violent criteria and Black-Code checklist to marginalize your fellow Black folks.*
- *Whiteness wants you to do its work of anti-blackness.*
- *Whiteness wants you to harm your own people and keep the cycle of violence spinning out of control.*
- *Whiteness is banking on your complicity to keep chaos and destruction raging within our community.*

Part of your healing work requires you to identify how you echo the evil acts of white violence and stop being the master's puppet. Part of your healing work requires you to understand how you strengthen the trauma bond, and to instead fight every day to break free from its grueling grip. Part of your healing work requires you to forgive yourself for participating in the cycle of violence. Part of your healing work requires you to give and accept apologies from other Black folks who have harmed you with the master's tools. Part of your healing work requires you to hold other Black folks accountable with compassion and without causing harm. Part of your healing work requires you to break this multigenerational curse by teaching your children and loved ones to not use the master's tools against other Black folks. Part of your healing work requires you to know you have the right and the choice to not forgive other Black folks who have harmed you, and you can still release them with love. (It's important to understand, however, that an authentic release requires forgiveness.) Choose your own way to heal. Do it on your own terms for your own reasons. It does not matter how it gets done, just do it. This is water for the fire.

A trauma bond's fundamental component is a promise. The person (or system) you are in the trauma bond with frequently and repeatedly promises to stop or change their violent and abusive behavior. This promise is similar to the Honeymoon Phase I described when talking about the cycle of violence in Chapter 3: it always includes hope and a payoff. The promise is a manipulative tool to keep you bonded in the trauma. The abusive person or system keeps your hopes up by vowing to be better and do better, and may on occasion show a slight improvement in their ability to alter behaviors. Yet there is no real commitment or urgency to make a dramatic and swift transformation. You hold on to the hope for change. It doesn't happen. The wounding is expanded, and although you know you need to release yourself from this bond, your mind and heart can't get in alignment to escape it.

This is because trauma bonds have three strangling elements that keep you from cutting the rope: intensity, complexity, and inconsistency. The abuse or violence demonstrated by the traumatizer is insidious and unpredictable. The abuse is often hard to recognize unless it's straight-up physical abuse, but most times the traumatizer is playing mind games, and it's hard to identify which games are being played. And because the traumatizer is manipulative and slick, they vacillate between acting out violence and acting like they care.

CHAPTER TEN | SEPARATION FOR LIBERATION

My late grandmother used to say, "If it were a snake, it would have bitten you." What she meant is the snake (the problem or truth) is staring you in the face, but you are so busy looking elsewhere, or are so preoccupied with other issues, you can't see it. And now the snake has the opportunity to bite you. Listen, the beast is staring you right in the eyes. Can you see it? It's slithering all around your feet, but you're too busy putting bounties on other Black folks' heads and monitoring your invisible checklist. In other words, the beast is hunting you, and you're hunting other Black folks. The Weapons of Whiteness are the snake you cannot see, and you also can't see how you use those weapons against other Black folks.

Many Black folks live and operate stuck between two trauma bonds: wounded by whiteness, and wounded by our own folks. Some die there. You don't have to live, operate, or die there. I want you to really examine how whiteness promises to change and do better, and I want you to understand it has no interest in, or intention of, doing either. Instead of optimistically holding on to the elusive promise of change by white folks, focus on changing yourself and on how you engage with other Black folks.

In addition to the trauma bond, I want to talk about another reason we use Weapons of Whiteness against each other. *Internalized oppression* is another tight fiber in the trauma bonds we experience, and can be defined as an oppressed group (Black folks) oppressing members of the same oppressed group (other Black folks) to be like or gain favor with the oppressor (white folks). Listen. It is anti-blackness! It's trying to gain greater proximity to whiteness while marginalizing your own people. As Brother Malcolm says, it is "a mask of self-hate and self-doubt." It is believing you are inferior. It is believing Black people are the problem, and that they are less worthy of dignity, respect, and appreciation.

Internalized oppression is dehumanization turned inward, and using Weapons of Whiteness against each other is dehumanization turned outward. And as Black folks trapped in two trauma bonds, we either act in by hating ourselves, or we act out by despising other Black folks, because they don't measure up to what whiteness says is right, honorable, worthy, or beautiful. When we *act in*, we self-abuse. When we *act out*, we are abusive. Internalized oppression is a vicious cycle of lose-lose, but some Black folks believe they are winning. The goal isn't to win, it is to resist the temptation to weaponize your internalized oppression. Then we can all get and live free.

We know whiteness uses all its methods and strategies to keep us from freedom and liberation. This may be a battle we will not win in our lifetime, but we must keep fighting against the system of white terrorism that strategically oppresses us. Separation in a way that works for you is a powerful tool. Earlier in this chapter, I suggested you purge whiteness from your living space and instead surround yourself with blackness; other examples of separation include buying from Black business owners, investing in Black companies, using Black spaces for events, and building the Black community. In what ways can you begin to separate to liberate? Make a list, work it consistently, and teach other Black folks how to use the power of separation. The goal is to get and live free, and to help other Black folks get and live free. Staying intertwined in the trauma bonds will not liberate us. Healing is a way out.

So, how do you know if you need healing? I believe we all need to heal in one way or another. Here are some signs or indicators that you need to either start your healing journey or deepen your current healing work. These behaviors are ones in which you are either *acting in* (self-abuse) or *acting out* (harming other Black people):

- *Past mistakes you cannot relinquish*
- *Insecurities you project onto other people*
- *Self-limiting beliefs and/or self-sabotage*
- *Constant critiquing of self and others*
- *Sarcasm, bitterness, and being petty*
- *Vindictiveness and revenge-seeking*
- *Thriving on creating chaos*
- *Persistent envy*
- *Instant dislike of someone because of their skin color*
- *Perpetual gossiping and the need to get all the tea*

Healing happens when your thoughts and feelings are no longer tied to a person or situation that harmed you. Deep and lasting healing happens when your way of being, living, and navigating your life is not dependent on whether someone else changes or not. Healing happens when you set yourself free from what ails you. Healing happens when you no longer put out bounties on Black people. Healing happens when you refuse to operate under the guidance of Black Codes and checklists. Healing happens when you can see the wounds of other Black folks because they look much like your own. Healing happens when you choose to hold Black folks accountable instead of dragging them into destruction.

DRAGGING AND ACCOUNTABILITY?
What's the Difference?

DRAGGING	ACCOUNTABILITY
Addresses the person	Addresses the behavior
About exposure	About responsibility
Can be vindictive	Focus on reconciliation
Seeks to also embarrass	Seeks ownership
May seek to destroy	Seeks a goal of repair
Punishment	Consequence
Can be performative	Doesn't need an audience
May not end in solutions	Seeks to resolve
Rarely seeks apology	Seeks atonement
Vengeance	Repentance
Can rally other people	Doesn't require others
Name calling and degradation	Refrains from defamation
Ego driven	Reparation driven
Lose/Lose	Hopeful for a Win/Win

I know you won't like or get along with all Black people. You won't be able to have a relationship with every Black person; in fact, it's unrealistic to believe you have to be in relationship with someone just because they are Black. And if a particular Black person is not a good fit for you, you can release them with love, and do no harm. This means we can cut ties and walk away while refusing to bash them, discredit them, or retaliate against them.

Listen. We can embody both accountability and love in so many ways; here are a few for you to think about:

- *We can be in community with each other even if we dislike one another. This means we can still go to the cookout even though there are Black folks there we don't like or who don't like us.*
- *We can love each other from a distance. This means we can set boundaries, not allow other Black folks to infect us with their toxicity, and still have love and compassion for them.*
- *We can choose to not let folks sit at our tables, but still help them get food to eat. This means we can determine with whom we commune and collaborate without blocking the coins other Black folks are trying to get.*
- *We can end relationships without bickering and gossip. This means we can stop using triangulation against each other: just because you had a falling out with a Black person should not mean I am obligated to fall out with or cancel them to still be your friend.*
- *We can show each other compassion and grace. This means we understand other Black people are trapped in the fire with us. Some unknowingly and others willingly, and we can show them grace when they try to spread the fire.*
- *We can set boundaries for each other AND expect them to be respected. This means when those boundaries are ignored, we can pick up the phone to*

- *create reconciliation instead of blasting each other's flame-throwing behavior on social media.*
- *We can understand we do not have the right to project our pain onto other Black folks. This means just because you are hurting, you do not have permission to hurt other Black folks and then hide behind your wounding.*
- *We can agree to disagree without demonizing one another. This means you get to do you, and I get to do me.*
- *We can choose to forgive and forget. This means we let go of our need for apologies before we heal our wounds.*
- *We can appreciate each other even if we don't like one another. This means you may not roll with someone, but you do not have to roll over them.*
- *We can dislike someone else's way of doing what they do, but we don't have to tear them down to lift ourselves up. This means there is more than one way to get this collective justice and liberation work done.*

Embodying a spirit of accountability and love is harder than throwing shade, stoking the fire, and dragging people for filth. It takes more courage to heal than to hate. We must lay down our Weapons of Whiteness and pick up the tools of accountability and love. We will never escape this burning house and be liberated as long as we allow ourselves to be pawns in white folks' gruesome game of dehumanizing and destroying blackness. We must refuse to strengthen the master's house, and we must starve the beast that hunts us. It may sound cliché, but love can conquer all. That's why I often say justice is love.

White folks may never love us, but we must love ourselves. We must love each other and protect each other. We must break the trauma bond we have with whiteness, we must stop weaponizing our internalized oppression, and we must separate to liberate. We must dismantle and destroy the Black Codes, and we must shred the checklists. We must exorcise our inner Beckys and Brads. We must extinguish the fire to set ourselves free without blocking our fellow Black people's escape, and we must be relentless about healing and allowing others to heal. You *can* do all these things. *We* can do all these things. And we must. We must live free and die trying. This is our collective work to do with accountability and love, so let's get busy and get to work until we take our last breath.

1 Corinthians 13:4-8

Love is patient, love is kind. It does not envy, it does not boast, it is not proud. It does not dishonor others, it is not self-seeking, it is not easily angered, it keeps no record of wrongs. Love does not delight in evil but rejoices with the truth. It always protects, always trusts, always hopes, always perseveres.

Love never fails.

LAY DOWN YOUR WEAPONS

WHITE SILENCE: When white folks hide behind their white privilege to refuse to speak up about racism.

In what ways are you being silent about the pain and suffering of Black folks who are different from you?

_____

_____

_____

_____

WHITE PERFORMATIVE APOLOGY: When white folks have been called out or critiqued on their use of a Weapon of Whiteness, and they use a scripted apology to look good, yet withdraw or lash out behind the scenes.

When you wield the Weapons of Whiteness, are you apologizing from a script? How can you show more humility with the Black folks you harm?

_____

_____

_____

_____

WHITE ROBOTISM: When white folks engage with Black and Brown folks with little or no emotion and/or with no genuine cellular connection.

What "types" of Black folks have you detached from? Why? How can you show more genuine care and empathy for them?

_____

_____

_____

_____

WHITE FLIGHT: When white folks dramatically increase their distance from Black and Brown folks to avoid contact.

In what ways have you separated yourself from the Black struggle?

_____

_____

_____

_____

How are you avoiding dealing with toxic whiteness and anti-blackness within the Black community?

_____

_____

_____

_____

_____

_____

How can you connect deeper to the Black struggle and engage in ways that help all Black folks get free?

_____

_____

_____

_____

_____

_____

WE DON'T HAVE TO LIKE EACH OTHER TO BE IN COMMUNITY, BUT WE CAN LOVE EACH OTHER AND DO NO HARM.

CATRICE M. JACKSON

AFTERWORD

Both parts of this chapter's quote are true, and they can exist simultaneously. There is no perfect or right strategy for Black unification and Black liberation, and that's due to our never-ending wounding from whiteness. The trauma we experience from whiteness and the trauma we create for each other keep us trapped in a perpetual cycle of violence. We exist in a space of constant fight, flight, and freeze, leaving little or no room for compassion, grace, healing, or joy. And just as I tell white folks, it's going to take a lifetime to rid ourselves of toxic whiteness and anti-blackness. This must be our most pressing call to action, and we must prioritize it and make it the center of our attention and intention, because fighting, fleeing, and freezing will not promote our healing, and those actions sure won't liberate us.

We love to holler, "We all we got," but do we really believe it? Truthfully, we are all we got, and we got to start living it. I will be the first to say I have yet to master this truth, so I work on being consistent with my thoughts by showing up in what I call the *"Catriceology Way."* The Catriceology Way is my personal strategy to be a conscious conduit for Black unification and Black liberation. In this Afterword, I share the top six personal commitments I have made to Black people and how I walk out those commitments.

1. GIVE BLACK PEOPLE COMPASSION AND GRACE

White terrorism and anti-blackness are baked into America's foundation, and so is our history of forgiving white folks. Hell, Black people have been forced to forgive them or suffer dire consequences for four hundred years. Forgiving white folks for their violence is a form of self-abuse we have been conditioned to commit. Isn't it bad enough we have to endure their violence? Being forced or trained to also have to forgive them for it is straight-up sinister. It's abusive, and after centuries of conditioning, it's now second nature for us. I have chosen to shift my capacity for compassion and grace to Black people. I especially reserve those attributes for them. White folks don't automatically receive compassion and grace from me; they have to earn them. And white people who don't value and appreciate my compassion and grace lose them.

My compassion and grace for Black folks look like me being more patient with them, forgiving them for their ignorance, ignoring comments I'm willing to let slide, and not holding grudges when they harm me. I don't always do this, and when I do, I don't always do it perfectly. That's because like you, I'm on my own personal journeys of ridding myself from toxic whiteness and anti-blackness and working to be a better human being.

How will you show Black people more compassion and grace?

_____

_____

_____

_____

2. TAKE NO SHIT AND DO NO HARM

Just because I offer Black people more compassion and grace than I do white people, it does not mean I'm willing to be a pushover or a doormat. Just like you, I deserve to set boundaries and have them respected. When people do not want to respect my boundaries, then it is not worth my time to have those people in my life. I receive the most attacks from white women; the group I receive the second highest amount of harm from is Black women. And if I am honest, they are the group of people I've knowingly and unknowingly caused the most harm to. This is because Black women have been taught to work against each other. We have been taught to compete with one another, and we have been conditioned to hate on each other.

We must undo this learning. We must teach ourselves, for the first time, to love each other in spite of our differences and conflicts. We have to stop competing and learn to collaborate with each other, and when we cannot collaborate, then we must do no harm. I believe in taking no shit and doing no harm. We can disagree and still love one another, and that's what I try to do every day. I give Black people a lot of compassion and grace, and even when they come for me, I don't seek revenge in any way. Ever.

What boundaries do you need to set, and what commitments do you need to make with yourself, so you can take no shit and do no harm?

_____

_____

3. RELEASE PEOPLE WITH LOVE

I must say I have mastered releasing people with love. When I say "release," I mean let people go emotionally, physically, and socially. Especially on social media. As soon as I realize another Black person doesn't mean me well, isn't good for my mental health, and/or they've made it very clear they have no interest in engaging with me or valuing our connection, I release them. When people don't appreciate my presence, I allow them to enjoy my absence. Most times I just go away quietly and stop engaging with them. Sometimes I give compassion and grace for too long, and then it takes me longer to release a person. But once I release, they are released. On a few occasions, I have agreed to let them back in, but in most cases another release happens shortly thereafter.

It is okay to release people. We are not all going to agree with, get along with, and/or like each other, and that is perfectly fine if we can release each other with love. By "with love," I mean just let them go and wish them well. No dragging. No smear campaigns. No gossiping. No vendettas or revenge. Nothing. Let them go and keep it moving. "With love" means you wish them no harm, and you hope they prosper and thrive. "With love" also means you love yourself enough to release whatever is heavy and weighing down your spirit. Sometimes it is necessary to let folks know you are releasing them, and other times you should just walk away without making a big scene. Each person you release requires a unique approach. But do not hold grudges. Don't stay connected if people are toxic, refuse to respect your boundaries, treat you like you don't matter, and/or fail to treat you with dignity and respect. Release them with love.

What does releasing people with love look like for you?

_____

_____

_____

_____

4. KNOW WHO IS WITH YOU VERSUS WHO IS FOR YOU

I am still perfecting this commitment. It is important to be able to quickly discern who is with you versus who is *for* you. People who are *with* you are just that: they are with you for the benefits their association with you brings. They are folks who want to be close to you for some type of advantage or perk. They want to gain access to your thoughts, ideas, plans, people, resources, and perceived clout. People who are with you want to be in your presence for personal gain, not mutual benefit. They often have hidden motives. In the beginning, they often appear very interested in you, are quite supportive, will shower you with compliments, and give you lots of pats on the back. They often present as a "real" friend, but soon they either go silent and/or the sweet behaviors turn salty. They stop engaging. They throw shade. Or they straight-up start dragging your name. This is often the result of either their motives not being met, and/or your realization they are not really *for* you.

Because when people are *for* you, their only motive is they genuinely care for and like you. They have no hidden agendas. They are not looking to gain anything but your friendship. People who are for you believe in and practice reciprocity in relationships. They know how to give and take. They easily give you the same (or similar) energy and support you give them.

The only things they truly want for you is for you to thrive and be successful, and they are often willing to help you achieve your goals. Folks who are for you love you, whether you have something to give them or not, or whether they have something to gain or not, by being your friend. People who are for you are the ones to keep around. They are real friends. The sooner you can discern this about people, the less trauma and stress you'll experience.

What are the signs that tell you someone is for you?

_____

_____

_____

_____

5. LET PEOPLE EAT EVEN IF IT'S NOT AT YOUR TABLE

Everyone deserves to eat. Including people you don't like or get along with. No matter how much I may not like or get along with another Black person, I am committed to doing no harm, especially by trying to block their ability to survive and thrive. This means I don't slander their name, and I don't do anything else that would prevent them from healing or getting what they need to thrive in life. Your table is not the only table from which folks can eat. And if for some reason you choose to not feed someone or let them sit at your table (be in community with you), don't try to stop them from creating their own table or eating at someone else's. I have personally experienced a Black woman who tried to block the bounty by discrediting my name. What I know is she cannot block blessings that are mine. I believe whatever is meant for me is truly meant for me, even if people may try to prevent me from getting it.

When you release people with love from your table, you do not block their bounty or try to make them starve. Conversely, releasing people with love allows for good karma to come your way. It is the law of reciprocity. When you do other people dirty, that dirt will come back to you in one way or another. I know it's sometimes hard to release folks with love—with the hope they can create or find another table—but the more you do it, the better you get at it. And the better you become as a person. Try it. Often.

If there is someone you don't want eating at your table, how can you make sure they are still able to eat?

_____

_____

_____

_____

6. CHOOSE ACCOUNTABILITY AND LOVE

When conflicts arise between me and other Black people, my first thought is to act with accountability and love. In my opinion, accountability is not a bad thing, and when it is done with intention and care, it can save many relationships and friendships that are on the brink of breaking. When conflicts arise, use accountability and love to address the person's behavior, not the person. Accountability is about holding people responsible by requesting that they not only take ownership of their behavior, but they also create a plan to reconcile their offense.

Accountability may or may not include the goal of remaining connected; however, atonement is definitely a desired outcome. When you hold someone accountable with love, there is no need for an audience or public display of dragging. You don't need to bring anyone else into the situation either, unless they are directly involved. Just keep the focus on you and the person who caused harm. When you hold someone accountable with love, there is no need for name calling, defamation, or destruction. Love does not use Weapons of Whiteness. Love seeks repentance. Love is hopeful. Love seeks resolve. Love is a win/win.

When others hurt us, it's hard to choose love. I don't always choose it, but I'm getting better at doing so more consistently. When we pick up the Weapons of Whiteness and use them on one another, those are not acts of love, those are the master's tools. And we will never dismantle the master's house by using his violence against each other. Using accountability and love with each other opens the pathway for all of us to heal. This is another way we rid ourselves from toxic whiteness. This is another way we bring about freedom and liberation.

What are some situations you're currently dealing with for which you need to choose accountability and love?

_____

_____

_____

We really are all we got. Although we can dislike each other and still be in community with each other, I am hoping what I have shared in this book will help you feel more genuine and consistent affection for your fellow Black people. Regardless, being in community is key, so that all of us can get free and be liberated once and for all from toxic whiteness. This is the Catriceology Way, and maybe this strategy and its commitments will help you while you create your own way. One last thing: I hope you always choose Blackness. I hope you choose it even when it doesn't choose you. Because we all we got!

I love you!

In solidarity.

> *"It is our duty to fight for our freedom.*
> *It is our duty to win.*
> *We must love each other and support each other.*
> *We have nothing to lose but our chains."*
>
> —Assata Shakur, *Assata: An Autobiography*

RESOURCES

WILLIE LYNCH LETTER

"The William Lynch speech is an address purportedly delivered by a certain William Lynch (or Willie Lynch) to an audience on the bank of the James River in Virginia in 1712 regarding control of slaves within the colony. The letter purports to be a verbatim account of a short speech given by a slave owner, in which he tells other slave masters that he has discovered the 'secret' to controlling black slaves by setting them against one another. The document has been in print since at least 1970, but first gained widespread notice in the 1990s, when it appeared on the Internet. Since then, it has often been promoted as an authentic account of slavery during the 18th century, though its inaccuracies and anachronisms have led historians to conclude that it is a hoax."

—Wikipedia contributors, "William Lynch speech,"
Wikipedia, The Free Encyclopedia

The Willie Lynch Letter is included here in its entirety, with anachronisms and misspellings intact.

THE MAKING OF A SLAVE!

Gentlemen:

I greet you here on the bank of the James River in the year of our Lord one thousand seven hundred and twelve. First, I shall thank you, the gentlemen of the Colony of Virginia, for bringing me here. I am here to help you solve some of your problems with slaves. Your invitation reached me on my modest plantation in the West Indies, where I have experimented with some of the newest and still the oldest methods for control of slaves. Ancient Rome's would envy us if my program is implemented.

As our boat sailed south on the James River, named for our illustrious King, whose version of the Bible we cherish, I saw enough to know that your problem is not unique. While Rome used cords of wood as crosses for standing human bodies along its highways in great numbers, you are here using the tree and the rope on occasions. I caught the whiff of a dead slave hanging from a tree, a couple miles back. You are not only losing valuable stock by hangings, you are having uprisings, slaves are running away, your crops are sometimes left in the fields too long for maximum profit, You suffer occasional fires, your animals are killed.

Gentlemen, you know what your problems are; I do not need to elaborate. I am not here to enumerate your problems, I am here to introduce you to a method of solving them. In my bag here, I have a foolproof method for controlling your black slaves. I guarantee every one of you that if installed correctly it will control the slaves for at least 300 hundred years. My method is simple. Any member of your family or your overseer can use it. I have outlined a number of differences among the slaves and make the differences bigger. I use fear, distrust and envy for control.

These methods have worked on my modest plantation in the West Indies and it will work throughout the South. Take this simple little list of differences and think about them. On top of my list is "age" but it's there only because it starts with an "A." The second is "COLOR" or shade, there is intelligence, size, sex, size of plantations and status on plantations, attitude of owners, whether the slaves live in the valley, on a hill, East, West, North, South, have fine hair, course hair, or is tall or short. Now that you have a list of differences, I shall give you an outline of action, but before that, I shall assure you that distrust is stronger than trust and envy stronger than adulation, respect or admiration. The Black slaves after receiving this indoctrination shall carry on and will become self refueling and self generating for hundreds of years, maybe thousands. Don't forget you must pitch the old black Male vs. the young black Male, and the young black Male against the old black male. You must use the dark skin slaves vs. the light skin slaves, and the light skin slaves vs. the dark skin slaves. You must use the female vs. the male. And the male vs. the female. You must also have you white servants and overseers distrust all Blacks. It is necessary that your slaves trust and depend on us. They must love, respect and trust only us. Gentlemen, these kits are your keys to control. Use them. Have your wives and children use them, never miss an opportunity. If used intensely for one year, the slaves themselves will remain perpetually distrustful of each other. Thank you, gentlemen.

LET'S MAKE A SLAVE!

It was the interest and business of slave holders to study human nature, and the slave nature in particular, with a view to practical results. I and many of them attained astonishing proficiency in this direction. They had to deal not with earth, wood and stone, but with men and by every regard they had for their own safety and prosperity they needed to know the material on which they were to work. Conscious of the injustice and wrong they were every hour perpetuating and knowing what they themselves would do. Were they the victims of such wrongs? They were constantly looking for the first signs of the dreaded retribution. They watched, therefore with skilled and practiced eyes, and learned to read with great accuracy, the state of mind and heart of the slave, through his sable face. Unusual sobriety, apparent abstractions, sullenness and indifference indeed, any mood out of the common was afforded ground for suspicion and inquiry.

Let us make a slave. What do we need? First of all we need a black nigger man, a pregnant nigger woman and her baby nigger boy. Second, we will use the same basic principle that we use in breaking a horse, combined with some more sustaining factors. What we do with horses is that we break them from one form of life to another that is we reduce them from their natural state in nature. Whereas nature provides them with the natural capacity to take care of their offspring, we break that natural string of independence from them and thereby create a dependency status, so that we may be able to get from them useful production for our business and pleasure.

CARDINAL PRINCIPLES FOR MAKING A NEGRO

For fear that our future Generations may not understand the principles of breaking both of the beast together, the nigger and the horse. We understand that short range planning economics results in periodic economic chaos; so that to avoid turmoil in the economy, it requires us to have breath and depth in long range comprehensive planning, articulating both skill sharp perceptions. We lay down the following principles for long range comprehensive economic planning. Both horse and niggers is no good to the economy in the wild or natural state. Both must be broken and tied together for orderly production. For orderly future, special and particular attention must be paid to the female and the youngest offspring. Both must be crossbred to produce a variety and division of labor. Both must be taught to respond to a peculiar new language. Psychological and physical instruction of containment must be created for both.

We hold the six cardinal principles as truth to be self evident, based upon the following the discourse concerning the economics of breaking and tying the horse and the nigger together, all inclusive of the six principles laid down about. NOTE: Neither principle alone will suffice for good economics. All principles must be employed for orderly good of the nation. Accordingly, both a wild horse and a wild or nature nigger is dangerous even if captured, for they will have the tendency to seek their customary freedom, and in doing so, might kill you in your sleep. You cannot rest. They sleep while you are awake, and are awake while you are asleep. They are dangerous near the family house and it requires too much labor to watch them away from the house. Above all, you cannot get them to work in this natural state. Hence both the horse and the nigger must be broken; that is breaking them from one form of mental life to another. Keep the body take the mind! In other words break the will to resist. Now the breaking process is the same for both the horse and the nigger, only slightly varying in degrees. But as we said before, there is an art in long range economic planning. You must keep your eye and thoughts on the female and the offspring of the horse and the nigger. A brief discourse in offspring development will shed light on the key to sound economic principles. Pay little attention to the generation of original breaking, but concentrate on future generations.

Therefore, if you break the female mother, she will break the offspring in its early years of development and when the offspring is old enough to work, she will deliver it up to you, for her normal female protective tendencies will have been lost in the original breaking process. For example take the case of the wild stud horse, a female horse and an already infant horse and compare the breaking process with two captured nigger males in their natural state, a pregnant nigger woman with her infant offspring. Take the stud horse, break him for limited containment.

Completely break the female horse until she becomes very gentle, whereas you or anybody can ride her in her comfort. Breed the mare and the stud until you have the desired offspring. Then you can turn the stud to freedom until you need him again. Train the female horse where by she will eat out of your hand, and she will in turn train the infant horse to eat out of your hand also. When it comes to breaking the uncivilized nigger, use the same process, but vary the degree and step up the pressure, so as to do a complete reversal of the mind. Take the meanest and most restless nigger, strip him of his clothes in front of the remaining male niggers, the female, and the nigger infant, tar and feather him, tie each leg to a different horse faced in opposite directions, set him a fire and beat both horses to pull him apart in front of the remaining nigger. The next step is to take a bull whip and beat the remaining nigger male to the point of death, in front of the female and the infant. Don't kill him, but put the fear of God in him, for he can be useful for future breeding.

THE BREAKING PROCESS OF THE AFRICAN WOMAN

Take the female and run a series of tests on her to see if she will submit to your desires willingly. Test her in every way, because she is the most important factor for good economics. If she shows any sign of resistance in submitting completely to your will, do not hesitate to use the bull whip on her to extract that last bit of resistance out of her. Take care not to kill her, for in doing so, you spoil good economic. When in complete submission, she will train her off springs in the early years to submit to labor when the become of age. Understanding is the best thing. Therefore, we shall go deeper into this area of the subject matter concerning what we have produced here in this breaking process of the female nigger. We have reversed the relationship in her natural uncivilized state she would have a strong dependency on the uncivilized nigger male, and she would have a limited protective tendency toward her independent male offspring and would raise male off springs to be dependent like her. Nature had provided for this type of balance. We reversed nature by burning and pulling a civilized nigger apart and bull whipping the other to the point of death, all in her presence. By her being left alone, unprotected, with the male image destroyed, the ordeal caused her to move from her psychological dependent state to a frozen independent state. In this frozen psychological state of independence, she will raise her male and female offspring in reversed roles.

For fear of the young males life she will psychologically train him to be mentally weak and dependent, but physically strong. Because she has become psychologically independent, she will train her female off springs to be psychological independent. What have you got? You've got the nigger women out front and the nigger man behind and scared. This is a perfect situation of sound sleep and economic. Before the breaking process, we had to be alertly on guard at all times. Now we can sleep soundly, for out of frozen fear his woman stands guard for us. He cannot get past her early slave molding process. He is a good tool, now ready to be tied to the horse at a tender age. By the time a nigger boy reaches the age of sixteen, he is soundly broken in and ready for a long life of sound and efficient work and the reproduction of a unit of good labor force. Continually through the breaking of uncivilized savage nigger, by throwing the nigger female savage into a frozen psychological state of independence, by killing of the protective male image, and by creating a submissive dependent mind of the nigger male slave, we have created an orbiting cycle that turns on its own axis forever, unless a phenomenon occurs and re shifts the position of the male and female slaves. We show what we mean by example. Take the case of the two economic slave units and examine them closely.

THE NIGGER MARRIAGE

We breed two nigger males with two nigger females. Then we take the nigger males away from them and keep them moving and working. Say one nigger female bears a nigger female and the other bears a nigger male. Both nigger females being without influence of the nigger male image, frozen with an independent psychology, will raise their offspring into reverse positions. The one with the female offspring will teach her to be like herself, independent and negotiable (we negotiate with her, through her, by her, we negotiate her at will). The one with the nigger male offspring, she being frozen with a subconscious fear for his life, will raise him to be mentally dependent and weak, but physically strong, in other words, body over mind. Now in a few years when these two offspring's become fertile for early reproduction we will mate and breed them and continue the cycle. That is good, sound, and long range comprehensive planning.

WARNING: POSSIBLE INTERLOPING NEGATIVES

Earlier we talked about the non economic good of the horse and the nigger in their wild or natural state; we talked out the principle of breaking and tying them together for orderly production. Furthermore, we talked about paying particular attention to the female savage and her offspring for orderly future planning, then more recently we stated that, by reversing the positions of the male and female savages, we created an orbiting cycle that turns on its own axis forever unless a phenomenon occurred and resift and positions of the male and female savages. Our experts warned us about the possibility of this phenomenon occurring, for they say that the mind has a strong drive to correct and re-correct itself over a period of time if I can touch some substantial original historical base, and they advised us that the best way to deal with the phenomenon is to shave off the brute's mental history and create a multiplicity of phenomena of illusions, so that each illusion will twirl in its own orbit, something similar to floating balls in a vacuum.

This creation of multiplicity of phenomena of illusions entails the principle of crossbreeding the nigger and the horse as we stated above, the purpose of which is to create a diversified division of labor thereby creating different levels of labor and different values of illusion at each connecting level of labor. The results of which is the severance of the points of original beginnings for each sphere illusion. Since we feel that the subject matter may get more complicated as we proceed in laying down our economic plan concerning the purpose, reason and effect of crossbreeding horses and nigger, we shall lay down the following definition terms for future generations. Orbiting cycle means a thing turning in a given path. Axis means upon which or around which a body turns. Phenomenon means something beyond ordinary conception and inspires awe and wonder. Multiplicity means a great number. Sphere means a globe. Cross breeding a horse means taking a horse and breeding it with an ass and you get a dumb backward ass long headed mule that is not reproductive nor productive by itself.

Crossbreeding niggers mean taking so many drops of good white blood and putting them into as many nigger women as possible, varying the drops by the various tone that you want, and then letting them breed with each other until another cycle of color appears as you desire. What this means is this;

Put the niggers and the horse in a breeding pot, mix some assess and some good white blood and what do you get? You got a multiplicity of colors of ass backward, unusual niggers, running, tied to a backward ass long headed mule, the one productive of itself, the other sterile. (The one constant, the other dying, we keep the nigger constant for we may replace the mules for another tool) both mule and nigger tied to each other, neither knowing where the other came from and neither productive for itself, nor without each other.

CONTROL OF THE LANGUAGE

Crossbreeding completed, for further severance from their original beginning, we must completely annihilate the mother tongue of both the new nigger and the new mule and institute a new language that involves the new life's work of both. You know language is a peculiar institution. It leads to the heart of a people. The more a foreigner knows about the language of another country the more he is able to move through all levels of that society. Therefore, if the foreigner is an enemy of the country, to the extent that he knows the body of the language, to that extent is the country vulnerable to attack or invasion of a foreign culture. For example, if you take a slave, if you teach him all about your language, he will know all your secrets, and he is then no more a slave, for you can't fool him any longer. For example, if you told a slave that he must perform in getting out "our crops" and he knows the language well, he would know that "our crops" didn't mean "our crops" and the slavery system would break down, for he would relate on the basis of what "our crops" really meant. So you have to be careful in setting up the new language for the slaves would soon be in your house, talking to you "man to man" and that is death to our economic system. In addition, the definitions of words or terms are only a minute part of the process. Values are created and transported by communication through the body of the language. A total society has many interconnected value system. All the values in the society have bridges of language to connect them for orderly working in the society. But for these language bridges, these many value systems would sharply clash and cause internal strife or civil war, the degree of the conflict being determined by the magnitude of the issues or relative opposing strength in whatever form.

For example, if you put a slave in a hog pen and train him to live there and incorporate in him to value it as a way of life completely, the biggest problem you would have out of him is that he would worry you about provisions to keep the hog pen clean, or the same hog pen and make a slip and incorporate something in his language where by he comes to value a house more than he does his hog pen, you got a problem. He will soon be in your house.

WEAPONS OF WHITENESS INVENTORY

Toxic whiteness is full of *Weapons of Whiteness*™: conscious and unconscious behaviors and words used to lethally deny your existence, stifle your spirit, silence your voice, and paralyze your progress. White folks learn and acquire this assaultive arsenal of weapons, which is directly and vicariously taught and passed on by white mothers, grandmothers, sisters, and aunts. White folks have been recklessly and unapologetically discharging these weapons against Black and Brown folks for centuries. This table inventories the top weapons and gives a brief description of each one.

Weapon of Whiteness Racism = White Terrorism	Catriceology Definition
1. **WHITE SILENCE**	When white folks hide behind their white privilege to refuse to speak up about racism.
2. **WHITE FRAGILITY**	When white folks are unable to engage in real conversations about racism without becoming emotionally discombobulated, lashing out, and/or withdrawing.

RESOURCES

Weapon of Whiteness Racism = White Terrorism	Catriceology Definition
3. **WHITE INNOCENCE** 	When white folks hide behind their white privilege to avoid having to acknowledge, understand, and/or be knowledgeable about racism and its effects. Also, to use ignorance as a justification for lack of action or response.
4. **WHITE DENIAL** 	When white folks refuse to admit to their racism and/or to acknowledge the systemic and structural racism and oppression of white terrorism.
5. **WHITE ENTITLEMENT** 	When white folks believe they are entitled to consume time, space, and conversations in order to be the center of attention, and when they expect to be taught, considered, and forgiven.
6. **WHITE TEARS** 	When white folks cry during discussions about racism, and/or claim they feel attacked, shamed, and hurt when their racism is pointed out or confronted.

Weapon of Whiteness Racism = White Terrorism	Catriceology Definition
7. **WHITE SUPERIORITY/ AUTHORITY** 	When white folks use their whiteness to dominate Black and Brown folks: speaking for and over, interrupting, taking up space, cutting in line, and dismissing their presence. Also, when white people think they are better than and/or know what is best for nonwhite people.
8. **WHITE DERAILMENT** 	When white folks engage in conversations about race and racism and shift the focus, insert a different topic, and/or minimize, justify, and rationalize racism.
9. **WHITESPLAINING** 	When white folks attempt to educate and/or speak for Black and Brown folks on topics of racism, oppression, and white terrorism.
10. **WHITE CENTERING** 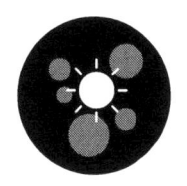	When white folks take up space, consume conversations, make everything about them, and talk over Black and Brown folks. Also, when white folks make whiteness and the feelings of white people the priority.

Weapon of Whiteness Racism = White Terrorism	Catriceology Definition
11. WHITE GUILT AND SHAME 	When white folks become consumed and paralyzed by guilt and shame, and then project it onto Black and Brown folks by shifting the blame.
12. WHITE COLLUSION 	When white folks willingly or unknowingly co-conspire with white terrorism and racism at the expense of Black and Brown folks. Also, when white folks choose white comfort over justice and equity for nonwhite people.
13. WHITE SAVIORISM 	When white folks demonstrate performative Allyship behavior for the sake of being seen as a "good" white person and/or as a way of showing pity. Also, when white folks attempt to "rescue" Black and Brown folks out of pity.
14. WHITE GASLIGHTING 	When white folks use silence, denial, and/or minimization to emotionally agitate Black and Brown folks before and after racial assaults.

Weapon of Whiteness Racism = White Terrorism	Catriceology Definition
15. WHITE TONE POLICING	When white folks tell Black and Brown folks how and when to speak about racism, oppression, and white terrorism—an extension of White Authority.
16. WHITE RIGHTEOUSNESS	When white people judge Black and Brown folks based on what is "white right" and demand right or wrong responses from them through the use of White Interrogation. These kinds of folks are more interested in being right (perfectionist) in their Allyship than being effective.
17. WHITE INTERROGATION	When white folks ask Black and Brown folks too many emotionally laborious DAMN questions, often as a derailment tactic.
18. WHITE FEMINISM	When white folks claim they support and advocate for ALL folks, yet fail or refuse to center, prioritize, and amplify Black and Brown folks and their needs and challenges.

Weapon of Whiteness Racism = White Terrorism	Catriceology Definition
19. WHITE PRIVILEGE	When white people have the luxury of not having to think about, talk about, or experience racism. Unearned safety, access, permission, credibility, inclusion, preference, approval, and protection because of whiteness.
20. WHITE PERFORMATIVE APOLOGY	When white folks have been called out or critiqued on their use of a Weapon of Whiteness, and they use a scripted apology to look good, yet withdraw or lash out behind the scenes.
21. WHITE INTELLECTUALIZING	When white folks fail to express empathy for the racism Black and Brown folks experience, and instead respond from a cognitive and intellectual space.
22. WHITE CLIPBOARDING	When white folks are obsessed with controlling the agency of Black and Brown folks, and do so by micromanaging their time, agendas, whereabouts, and schedules.

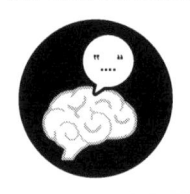

Weapon of Whiteness Racism = White Terrorism	Catriceology Definition
23. WHITE GAZE 	When white folks stare at Black and Brown folks with violent curiosity, lust, and/or disgust. Also, when white folks snoop into Black spaces to consume Black thoughts, ideas, and culture.
24. WHITE APATHY 	When white folks don't give a damn about Black and Brown folks and fail to ensure nonwhite lives are safe and protected.
25. WHITE TRIANGULATION 	When white folks try to pit one Black or Brown person against another Black or Brown person.
26. WHITE CODES 	When white folks use a set of conscious and unconscious rules, guidelines, standards, and expectations to try to control and deny the agency and sovereignty of Black folks.

Weapon of Whiteness Racism = White Terrorism	Catriceology Definition
27. WHITE FETISHIZATION	When white folks objectify, glorify, consume, and dehumanize the Black body for profit and pleasure.
28. WHITE FAVORITISM	When white folks enact anti-blackness by choosing which Black and Brown folks they will listen to, endorse, and support based on who will provide the most coddling, grace, and compassion.
29. WHITE EMBEZZLEMENT	When white folks steal intellectual property from Black and Brown folks to pawn off as their own for personal, social, and economic profit.
30. WHITE CONSUMPTION	When white folks consume blackness and Black and Brown people's energy and space for their own personal gain.

Weapon of Whiteness Racism = White Terrorism	Catriceology Definition
31. WHITE PADDY ROLLING 	When white folks act like slave patrols by policing Black bodies and reporting them to the "authorities" and/or making "citizen's arrests."
32. WHITE CO-SIGNING 	When white folks co-sign, co-conspire with, and collude with other white folks' racism.
33. WHITE ANTAGONISM 	When white folks agitate, irritate, and purposely trigger Black and Brown folks with racial comments and behaviors.
34. WHITE TERRORISM 	When white folks use Weapons of Whiteness to assault, insult, invalidate, silence, harm, and oppress Black and Brown folks.

Weapon of Whiteness Racism = White Terrorism	Catriceology Definition
35. WHITE GATEKEEPING 	When white folks assume false authority on what Black and Brown folks can or cannot access and do.
36. WHITE DOG WHISTLING 	When white folks use dangerous and coded language to passively incite violence against Black and Brown folks and/or to summon the lynch mob.
37. WHITE TATTLING 	When white folks ask to speak to the manager and/or call the police on Black and Brown folks.
38. WHITE LARCENY 	When white folks increase their proximity to Black and Brown folks and their cultures to appropriate, rape, rob, and steal from nonwhite folks.

Weapon of Whiteness Racism = White Terrorism	Catriceology Definition
39. WHITE MANIPULATION	When white folks use their whiteness or the benefits of whiteness to coerce Black or Brown folks into doing things they shouldn't or don't want to do.
40. WHITE POSITIVITY	When white folks weaponize positivity to minimize and excuse racial assaults and/or use spiritual bypassing to deflect and deny racist acts.
41. WHITE HELICOPTERING	When white folks hover around Black and Brown folks to be nosey and to micro-manage their actions and work.
42. WHITE BUSY-BODYING	When white folks are obsessed with being in Black and Brown spaces and discussions; in other words, inserting themselves where they are unwanted.

Weapon of Whiteness Racism = White Terrorism	Catriceology Definition
43. WHITE FLIGHT	When white folks dramatically increase their distance from Black and Brown folks to avoid contact.
44. WHITE ROBOTISM	When white folks engage with Black and Brown folks with little or no emotion and/or with no genuine cellular connection.
45. WHITE FALSE PRIDE	When white folks believe they are exceptional, distance themselves from white terrorism, and self-proclaim their Allyship.

TYPES OF BECKYS

Note that these Becky types apply to white men too, and then we call them Brads!

SUPER BECKY
A savior-complex Becky who is notorious for jumping into conversations about racism to Save-a-Black or Brown person without their consent.

BEGGING BECKY
A performative Becky who is always sniffing around, panting for pats on the back, and begging for Ally Cookies (accolades and praise).

WANNA-BE-BLACK BECKY
A Becky who loves to date Black folks, fetishizes Black folks, and appropriates AAVE to appear "woke."

TALK-TOO-DAMN-MUCH BECKY
A talkative, centering Becky who adds no value, validity, or validation in race talks.

KNOW-IT-ALL BECKY
A condescending, apathetic Becky who intellectualizes racism by using a cognitive approach to understanding and discussing racism.

LOVE-AND-LIGHT BECKY
An oblivious Becky who selfishly uses a sprinkling of love, light, and woo-woo talk to avoid facing her racism and to minimize your oppression.

WHINING-ASS BECKY
The most brittle Becky of all. She's perpetually hurt about anything and everything related to racism. She's a master of crying a river of White Tears.

OLE-THIEVING-ASS BECKY
A Becky who rapes and robs the culture of Black and Brown folks to create an identity so she can feel alive inside.

GET-ON-YOUR-NERVES BECKY
A Becky who just gets on your nerves. She's a combination of Talk-Too-Damn-Much Becky and Know-It-All Becky, and she will exhaust the hell out of you.

COWORKER BECKY
A Becky who smiles in your face and tries to sabotage your success at work.

BWAM (BUT WHAT ABOUT ME?) BECKY
A Becky whose favorite Weapon of Whiteness is White Centering. She becomes emotionally brittle and defensive when she is not getting all the attention.

WEAPONS FOR WINNING

(AGAINST BECKY AND BRAD)

Weapons for Winning and Amplifying Your Joy

These weapons for winning previously appeared in my books *The Becky Code* and *Unf*ckablewith*.

1. DARE to Speak:
When white folks DENY your truth, stories, and experiences, DARE to speak and call them out on their violation and violence. Of course, you must DISCERN whether this is a battle you're willing to engage in or not. If you decide it isn't, remember your silence will not protect you. If you fail to address Becky's and Brad's violence, they are likely to violate you again. Iyanla Vanzant says, *"We must call a thing a thing."* This means you must identify and name racism for what it is by calling it out explicitly as white terrorism.

2. DISOBEY the Expectations:
When white folks DEFEND their racism, they *expect* you to stay silent and to accept their manipulative, defensive rationale. They *expect* you to understand their "mistake." They *expect* you to talk nicely to them about your pain while they cause it. They *expect* you to pull them to the side and to not call them out publicly. They *expect* you to NOT shame them. They *expect* you to forgive them for their violence.

They *expect* you to watch your tone and to not be angry. They *expect* you to explain or teach them about racism. **DISOBEY ALL THESE EXPECTATIONS!**

- DO NOT let them take your kindness for weakness.
- DO NOT subdue your tone and voice. Remember what Zora Neale Hurston says: "If you are silent about your pain, they will kill you and say you enjoyed it."
- DO NOT feel the need to talk privately about their racism. They will abuse you behind closed doors.
- DO NOT let them manipulate you with declarations of shame and their white tears.
- You DO NOT have to forgive their violence.
- DO NOT waste your magic and emotional energy on educating them.
- Be angry and mad if you want to. You DO NOT need anyone's permission or approval to express your anger. (Don't stay angry, however, because doing so hurts only you.)
- DO NOT FOLLOW THEIR RULES OF ENGAGEMENT. DISOBEY EVERY TIME. For centuries, white folks have had the expectation that Black and Brown folks will follow their white rules and expectations. You don't have to!

3. DISCONTINUE the Dialogue

When white folks try to DERAIL the conversation about racism, know this is an intentional tactic used to avoid looking at their own racism. White folks get extremely uncomfortable when talking about racism, and they will try to create an intellectual and emotion distraction to avoid dealing with their passive or active role in racism and white terrorism. Instead of following them into the violent white abyss, call out their attempts to derail the conversation. At this point, Becky and Brad have made it clear they do not want to hear your truth, and they do not want to stop their racial violence. DETACH. It's time to DISCONTINUE dialoguing with them. This is not a battle you want to continue. This is the point where we give away our precious energy and power to antagonistic white folks who do not want to change. Walk away. You do not have to prove your humanity to them. They are NOT worth the agony.

4. DETOX and Delight

When white folks try to DESTROY your joy, say, *"Nah, not today, Becky! Not today, Brad!"* On some days, it is worth the fight to go into battle with Becky and Brad. But I want to encourage you to choose a different, more nourishing option instead on most days. When the need arises, then dare to speak, disobey the expectations, discontinue the dialogue, and demand to be heard and respected. And don't forget to maintain your magic by detoxing yourself from the Beckery and the Bradery. You are here for a very special reason and a divine purpose. Don't let Becky and Brad hijack your destiny! Taking care of yourself and making YOU priority number one is essential.

WE ALL WE GOT | UNF*CKABLEWITH

This poem first appeared in my book *Unf*ckablewith*. Although it is addressed to Black women, its message is for all Black people.

I can't breathe.
I can't breathe.
I can't breathe!
Too loud.
Too dark.
Too light.
Too bossy.
I can't breathe.
Too independent.
Too ratchet.
Too bougie.
Too ghetto.
I can't breathe.
No, you can't touch my hair.
No, I ain't your mammy.
No, I won't be your footstool.
Damn, I can't breathe.
I can't breathe.
Too strong.
Too bold.
I'm tired.

I can't breathe.
Stop touching me.
Leave me alone.
No, I don't want to explain.
What the hell you looking at?
I can't breathe.
Can I just live?
White toxicity consuming all the space.
Get out of my way.
Damn, can I get a seat at the table?
Ain't I a woman?
Get off my neck!
*I can't f*cking breathe!*
I'm dying...
Yes, it's my real hair!
Get your hands off my mouth.
Stop silencing me.
I'm tired.
I can't breathe.
Yes, I'm angry.
Sick of folks pressuring me.
Do you hear me screaming?
No, I won't move out the way.
I don't owe you a smile.
I don't owe you shit!
Did you hear me say I can't breathe!
I'm tired of being woke.
Why are you staring at me?
I'm falling, y'all!
Do you hear me?

Do you see me?
I said I can't breathe!
I don't owe you nothing.
I'm not your negro!
I'm tired of shucking and jiving!
Whew…
I can't catch my breath.
I'm losing it.
So tired.
Stop touching my children.
What'd you say to me?
Watch my tone?
Damn.
Can I catch my breath?
I can't breathe. I can't freaking breathe!
I'm dying.
Can you see my pain?
No, I won't teach you.
I'm not a resource.
Can I just have some joy?
No, I won't wait my turn!
No, I won't shrink.
I'm drowning, y'all.
I'm tired.
You too, Sis?
You causing me pain, too?
Not you too, Black Woman.
It hurts!
Damn.
Ain't no safe place for Black women.

It's too much.
I can't take it.
Sick of shifting and shuffling.
My feet hurt.
I'm exhausted.
I can't breathe!
Damn, another Black person killed?
Stop killing us!
Does anybody care?
Who is going to protect us?
Stop bumping into me.
I do not have to concede.
No, I don't work here!
Why are you following me?
Do you see my tears?
I'm weak.
I'm overwhelmed!
Somebody help me!
Please!
Whew...
Whew...
I'm suffocating.
Gasp...
Silence...
Wait, Sis!
Keep breathing.
Don't you quit.
Don't you give up.
I got you.
Get up, Sis.

You are not alone.
I know your pain.
Your rage is justified.
Here, have some of my breath.
My strength.
Lean on me.
I got you.
Get up.
You can make it through this.
Let me carry you for a while.
I see you. I hear you.
Don't let them kill you!
Puff…
Puff…
Puff…
Sis.
Inhale.
Breathe.
C'mon, Sister.
You are a Queen.
Do you know who you are?
Puff…
Puff…
Puff…
You are valuable.
You matter.
I love you.
I need you.
You need you.
We need you.

C'mon, Sis.
I love you, Sis.
Don't give up.
There is royalty in your blood.
You got dreams to fulfill.
Breathe!
Breathe!
Breathe!
Your destiny is waiting for you.
You don't have to do it alone.
I know you're tired.
It's okay to be vulnerable.
I got you.
Puff...
Puff...
Puff...
Gasp...
Whew!
Whew!
Inhale...
Exhale...
You're breathing!
Inhale.
Open your eyes, Sis!
You can breathe.
Take a deep breath.
Hold on to me.
I got you.
Stand up.
Stand on the shoulders of your ancestors!

They are with you.
I am with you.
Breathe.
Breathe, Sis!
Rise up.
Rise up!
Yes!
That's right. You can do this!
Rise up, Sis!
From those ashes...
Don't let the fire consume you!
Yes, you're standing up!
Hold your head up.
Breathe!
Rise up!
Rise.
Up.

* * * * *

I don't know what kind of ashes you may be standing in right now.
I don't know the pain you might be experiencing.
I don't know your struggles and fears.
I don't know what you're going through.
But I do know this: you don't have to go through it alone.
I know you're valuable and you matter.
I know what the fire feels like.
I've been through storms, too.
I know your rage is justified.

I know the fire can consume you if you let it.
I know you can rise from your ashes.
I know you can become the fire.
I will go through the storm with you.
I will rage with you. I will become the fire with you.
I'm here with and for you.
I got you.
It's time to rise up, Sis!
*Rise up and go on this journey into the dimensions of Unf*ckablewith with me.*
It's time.
It's time to rise up into your Black Woman Badassery!
Let's go.

THREE POWERFUL STEPS FOR YOUR HEALING JOURNEY

These suggestions for healing first appeared in my book *Unf*ckablewith*.

1. **TELL YOURSELF THE TRUTH.**
   THE UNFILTERED. RAW. EXPLICIT TRUTH.
   - Tell yourself the truth.
   - You can't change what you're not willing to address, and you can't heal what you refuse to name.
   - By allowing whatever pain or hurt you have in your soul to remain, and telling yourself you're fine and it's okay, is to lie to yourself and be completely out of integrity and soul alignment.
   - The soul knows the truth, and therefore, this discomfort or dis-ease is stored in your body, not your mind.
   - The real wound is a soul wound, which means cognitive interventions will not be your most effective options for healing.

2. **CHOOSE HEALING**
   - The real work has to be done via body work, because that is where the trauma is housed: it lives in the body and reverberates into your emotions and mind.
   - Choose healing relentlessly and repeatedly. I want you to choose it like you choose to breathe. Choose

it like it is the most important thing you'll ever do in your lifetime, because it is. Choose yourself over everything. Choose your health and joy before you choose others. Choose life. Choose freedom. Choose liberation. Choose to be happy. Choose to be whoever the f*ck you want to be. Healing is not optional.

- There are many forms of body work, and you don't always need to pay someone for these services. A few therapeutic examples are massage, aromatherapy, acupuncture, cupping, yoga, hot stone therapy, reflexology, reiki, herbalism, meditation, and sound and color therapy. Others may include visualization, guided imagery, music and dance therapy, artistic expression, and of course, nutrition. Listen to your body and soul; they know what you need.

- If you choose to include mental health therapy as part of your healing work, it's critical you hire a therapist who is culturally competent and who understands the effects of racism and oppression on the lives of Black people. Before you hire someone, make sure they are not only doing their own anti-racism work, but that they also have a tangible anti-racism plan as part of their service provision.

- If you do not hire someone with these qualifications, and do not hire someone who uses a trauma-informed method of treatment, you will be retraumatized, and your soul wounds will be exacerbated. Please do your due diligence if you decide to pursue mental health services in your community.

3. DEFINE AND EMBODY LIBERATION AND REVOLUTION ON YOUR OWN TERMS

- You've mastered your ability to be resilient and strong, now it's time to master your healing and ability to thrive!
- You must live in your authenticity and in the truth that you are free and liberated. How you do it doesn't matter to me—I just want you to be *Unf*ckablewith!*
- My desire is for you to be unbothered and unapologetic, and that you will rise from the ashes into your Black Badassery.
- My additional hope for Black women is that you relentlessly activate your Black Girl Magic to resist, rise, revolutionize, and thrive.

50 WAYS TO BE MORE COURAGEOUS

Here are 50 tips for you to live more courageously, from my book *The Art of Fear-Free Living: Awaken the Geni(us) Within*.

1. Make a list of the things you need to forgive yourself for, and then, one by one, release the shame, guilt, and regret.
2. Identify the people in your life you need to forgive. Choose to do the work within your heart to forgive them.
3. Start a courage journal, write down all the things you want to do, and find creative ways to make them happen.
4. Choose the risks you can take now to be more courageous.
5. Remember not only the moments when you were wise and strong, but also how you were able to create success in those moments.
6. Make a list of the values and standards you want to live by, and start living by them.
7. Think about all the things you do that you don't like or want to do and create your "not to do" list. Be brave and just stop doing those things.
8. Use your fears to drive you toward your passion and purpose.
9. When you become aware of fear, remember that the awareness of fear is a signal that something is missing from your life.

10. See the same significance in feeding your soul as you do in feeding your body. Determine how you will feed your soul every day.
11. Check your emotional energy tank and determine who is filling it or causing you to run on fumes. Determine what you can do to remove the energy stealers in your life and do it.
12. Decide what you can do every day to move from surviving in life to thriving in your life.
13. Every time you feel fearful, ask yourself, "What is the worst that could happen if I do not face this fear, and what is the worst that could happen if I *do* face this fear?" You'll see you have more to lose by NOT facing your fears.
14. Remember, you have only two choices in life: be afraid and live afraid or be fearless and live courageously.
15. Instead of focusing your energy on your fears, focus your energy on how you can get the resources you need to conquer them.
16. Color the canvas of your life with vibrant, energetic, and happy people who can keep you inspired to master the art of fear-free living.
17. Remember that every day you have the choice to take down the old, dull, and gray canvas and put up a blank one to create your fearless life.
18. Know that your personal power is like a big eraser. You have the power to erase the negative thoughts about yourself, the past hurts that are keeping you stuck, and everything in your life that is causing you distress and misery.

19. As you begin to create a fear-free life, remember that you have the tools you need within you—you just have to seek them out and use them.

20. Be mindful to stay off autopilot. Instead, live each moment of your life fully awake.

21. Make it a personal priority to ask yourself every day, "What I need to face, and how can I face it not only with the resources I need, but also with ease and grace?

22. Be intentional in every moment. Engage only in activities and conversations that move you one step closer to your goals.

23. Remember that facing your fears is simply about taking risks. You must be willing to take some risks to get what you desire.

24. Create a vision board, and fill it up with words, pictures, and quotes that depict how you want to live your fearless life.

25. Create your fearless life dream team: a small group of dedicated, positive, and trustworthy people who believe in you and your dreams and who will help you bring them to life.

26. Be mindful to not make excuses or reasons for not doing something that can empower your life. Excuses are the doorway to failure.

27. When faced with a fear, instead of allowing yourself to worry and become paralyzed, seek out the resources to help you conquer the fear.

28. Be curious. When faced with a fear, ask yourself, "I wonder what would happen if I faced this fear?" Be still and listen for the answer that comes from your heart.

29. Make the choice to accept that you will have obstacles in your life and begin to see them as opportunities to strengthen yourself.

30. Instead of dreading facing your fears, wake up each day with gratitude and ask yourself, "How can I be brave today?" And then take action.

31. *Unsubscribe!* That's right; opt out of everything that does not fill your cup, fulfill you, serve your highest good, and/or take you one step closer to your highest self.

32. Surrender once a day. In the morning, surrender to the Universe and let God order your steps. In the evening, surrender again and release all the toxicity you've taken in during the day.

33. Choose to be struggle-free! Struggle brings pain and frustration, which are not worth paying for with your life.

34. Be accepting. Sometimes you've simply got to say, "It is what it is." Let it go and keep it moving.

35. Quit looking for the answers. Instead, let them just come to you, and enjoy life while you wait for the divine downloads to occur.

36. Trust yourself more. Trust that what you need will come. Trust that you know yourself better than anyone else. Stop fighting with yourself, and instead, just trust yourself.

37. Take action! Worrying, contemplating, agonizing, and analyzing are signs of struggle. Ask your heart and your soul whether you should act, and if you feel peace overcome you, then get out of your head and take action.

38. Learn how to filter out the background noise. The background noise is other people's opinions, demands, and requests. It's your life, do what you want to do, and make your own decisions.

39. Release the need to be right or perfect. There's no such thing as perfect, and you will never be right all the time. Instead, strive to be the best you can be without measuring yourself against anyone. Remember that being wrong means you're human.

40. When you stop judging others, you will learn to accept them for who they are. This allows you to begin to accept *yourself* just as you are.

41. Your past is a part of who you are, but it does not determine who you will become. Let go and be free or keep holding on and be miserable.

42. Take out a new canvas every day and start over. Yesterday is gone and is a memory. Tomorrow may never come and is a dream. Today is all you have and is a blessing.

43. Every day you have a choice to stay captive, or to be brave, take out your courage key, and unlock your life. Stop wallowing in "what if," and begin basking in your bravery.

44. Look for at least one opportunity each day to grow and evolve. Read a new book, write in your journal—it doesn't matter what you do, as long as it takes you one step closer to fearless living.

45. Get over yourself! Someone out there has it worse than you do. While you are indeed important, the world does not revolve around you.

46. Fearless living is about survival of the fittest. Either you change, grow, and evolve, or life will pass you by. Get up and get into your life.

47. You can't change everything in your life with one choice, but the choice to live fearlessly can make a dramatic change.

48. Choose to live deliciously! Write down your recipe for a delicious life on a real recipe card. Get creative and add in a little spice, passion, excitement, satisfaction, and zest, and you are sure to whip up a life that makes your mouth water.

49. Clock in and go to work! Living YOUR LIFE fearlessly is an inside job. It's the most important job you will ever have in your life. Go in early, work hard, take on extra projects, be on the leadership team, put in 100%, stay late, clock out, and start all over again. When you work this job like it's the only one, you'll ever have, the recognition, raises, and promotions are guaranteed.

50. Decide what you want, how you want to be, and how you want to live your life, and then get it, be it, and live it. The only thing keeping you from living a rewarding and fulfilling life is you. Tell your ego to get out of the way and allow your best version of yourself to reign in your life. It's your life—own it, create it, live it, and love it—fearlessly!

WRITING PROMPTS TO RISE FROM THE ASHES

Use these writing prompts to help you release and process your feelings around fighting both systemic racism and anti-blackness. My hope is that these prompts will allow you to focus more on your healing and joy. I believe it's not only possible, but also necessary and urgent, that each of us rise from the ashes!

How are you allowing life to just happen instead of actively creating it?

_____

_____

_____

_____

In what ways are you choosing to self-abuse and play the role of victim?

_____

_____

_____

_____

Who have been some of your teachers and what have you learned from them?

_____

_____

_____

_____

What life lessons do you keep repeating that you no longer want to repeat?

_____

_____

_____

_____

How do you truly feel about yourself?

_____

_____

_____

_____

What do you believe to be true about yourself?

_____

_____

_____

_____

Who do you need to forgive?

_____

_____

_____

_____

In what areas of your life do you need to take full responsibility and stop blaming others?

_____

_____

_____

_____

What kind of conditioning have you experienced that you want to unlearn?

_____

_____

_____

_____

What do you think your spiritual gifts are?

_____

_____

_____

_____

What would you like to see in the panoramic view of your life?

_____

_____

_____

_____

What will you focus on from this point on?

_____

_____

_____

_____

In what ways are you settling, struggling, and living in mediocrity?

_____

_____

_____

_____

Who do you want to be until you take your last breath?

_____

_____

_____

_____

In what ways have you heard God's voice but dismissed it or didn't believe it?

_____

_____

_____

_____

How would you like God to speak to you so you can take action?

_____

_____

_____

_____

What did you learn from your family and upbringing that you want to unlearn so you can break the cycle?

_____

_____

_____

_____

In what ways are you still living in the past?

_____

_____

_____

_____

How do you define success?

_____

_____

_____

_____

How do you define significance?

_____

_____

_____

_____

Are you average or extraordinary? Why?

_____

_____

_____

_____

In what ways are you seeking approval from others or waiting for their permission?

_____

_____

_____

_____

Who are you blaming and what are you blaming them for?

_____

_____

_____

_____

What is your personal purpose?

_____

_____

_____

_____

What is your global purpose?

_____

_____

_____

_____

What hunches, nudges, or whispers have you experienced that are leading you to your purpose?

_____

_____

_____

_____

What are some of your ego's favorite ways of sabotaging you?

_____

_____

_____

_____

Are you living a more fear-driven life or a more love-driven life, and in what ways?

_____

_____

_____

_____

In what ways do you best serve the world?

_____

_____

_____

_____

In what ways is your life cluttered?

_____

_____

_____

_____

What do you need to release and let go of?

_____

_____

_____

_____

In what ways are you creating your own suffering?

_____

_____

_____

_____

What do you need to tell the truth about?

_____

_____

_____

_____

What truth do you need to know so you can move forward?

_____

_____

_____

_____

How has being afraid affected your life?

_____

_____

_____

_____

What fears do you need or want to face?

_____

_____

_____

_____

How are you holding yourself back?

_____

_____

_____

_____

What bricks are on top of your lid?

_____

_____

_____

_____

How can you step up and be the leader of your own life?

_____

_____

_____

_____

What is the vision for your life?

_____

_____

_____

_____

What have you been thinking about doing that you are now willing to take action on?

_____

_____

_____

_____

What thinking errors (distorted thoughts) are keeping you stuck and unfulfilled in your life?

_____

_____

_____

_____

How have you been comparing your life to the lives of others?

_____

_____

_____

_____

Who are some people you know who show up, serve, and/or live a life like the one you desire?

_____

_____

_____

_____

If you were to reach out to those people and ask for support, what do you need from them?

_____

_____

_____

_____

When are you most inspired?

_____

_____

_____

_____

Can you hear your soul's undeniable messages? Why or why not?

_____

_____

_____

_____

In what ways are you dimming your light?

_____

_____

_____

_____

What would your life be like if you said a full-body "yes" to your significance?

_____

_____

_____

_____

In what ways have you been money-focused and money-driven?

_____

_____

_____

_____

What's your big mission in life?

_____

_____

_____

_____

How can you become more mission-driven?

_____

_____

_____

_____

Fear is a liar! How has fear lied to you?

_____

_____

_____

_____

What physical symptoms are you experiencing that are telling you it's time to let something go so you can move on?

_____

_____

_____

_____

How are you owning your life?

_____

_____

_____

_____

In what ways are you NOT owning your life?

_____

_____

_____

_____

How do you know when your soul is speaking?

_____

_____

_____

_____

In what ways do you lead with your ego?

_____

_____

_____

_____

What is your soul's calling?

_____

_____

_____

_____

What do you desire that is outside your comfort zone?

_____

_____

_____

_____

What are you willing to lose to gain everything you desire?

_____

_____

_____

_____

Who are the doubters and naysayers in your life?

_____

_____

_____

_____

Who are the destiny-seekers in your life?

_____

_____

_____

_____

What do you need to believe so you can go out and create magic in your life?

_____

_____

_____

_____

How would you describe what MORE looks like for you?

_____

_____

_____

_____

What special gifts do you have?

_____

_____

_____

_____

What kind of relationship do you have with money?

_____

_____

_____

_____

What lessons have you been taught about money?

_____

_____

_____

_____

How can you use your gifts to make money?

_____

_____

_____

_____

What signs do you see that are telling you it's time to make a move and/or experience MORE in your life?

_____

_____

_____

_____

What boundaries do you need to put in place so people will respect you and your time?

_____

_____

_____

_____

What do you BELIEVE you deserve?

_____

_____

_____

_____

What is missing from your life?

_____

_____

_____

_____

How do you plan to make a difference in the world?

_____

_____

_____

_____

What have you been chasing in life?

_____

_____

_____

_____

What have you been searching for?

_____

_____

_____

_____

When do you get your best ideas?

_____

_____

_____

_____

What do you do to slow down?

_____

_____

_____

_____

What would inner peace feel like for you?

_____

_____

_____

_____

In what ways is your life out of order?

_____

_____

_____

_____

How will you create harmony in your life?

_____

_____

_____

_____

What kind of dis-ease are you experiencing?

_____

_____

_____

_____

How would you describe your current self-love status?

_____

_____

_____

_____

What do you really value?

_____

_____

_____

_____

How would you describe the energy you bring with you?

_____

_____

_____

_____

What kind of energy do you WANT to bring with you?

_____

_____

_____

_____

How will you begin to love yourself better?

_____

_____

_____

_____

What kind of life would you like to wake up to every day?

_____

_____

_____

_____

You have greatness within you; do you know what it is?

_____

_____

_____

_____

What have you overcome that you should celebrate?

_____

_____

_____

_____

What is your big crazy dream?

_____

_____

_____

_____

How can audacity help you live your dream?

_____

_____

_____

_____

Who do you choose to be?

_____

_____

_____

_____

How would you describe what your best version of yourself looks and feels like?

_____

_____

_____

_____

What about yourself can you honor right now?

_____

_____

_____

_____

What do you love about yourself?

_____

_____

_____

_____

How would you describe your bliss?

_____

_____

_____

_____

What will you do to follow your bliss?

_____

_____

_____

_____

Who is in your corner?

_____

_____

_____

_____

What type of people do you need to add to your circle?

_____

_____

_____

_____

How has your current level of Emotional Intelligence served you? How has it hindered you?

_____

_____

_____

_____

What makes you feel alive inside?

_____

_____

_____

_____

Who or what is creating misery in your life?

_____

_____

_____

_____

How are YOU creating misery in your life?

_____

_____

_____

_____

What kind of magic do you want to create?

_____

_____

_____

_____

What multidimensional magic lives within you?

_____

_____

_____

_____

In what ways are you speaking DEATH into your life?

_____

_____

_____

_____

In what ways are you speaking LIFE into your life?

_____

_____

_____

_____

What excites your spirit?

_____

_____

_____

_____

What do you seek?

_____

_____

_____

_____

What do you want to do every day for the rest of your life?

_____

_____

_____

_____

What are you here to do?

_____

_____

_____

_____

What is your true calling?

_____

_____

_____

_____

How would you describe what a meaningful life would look like for you?

_____

_____

_____

_____

How do you want to feel for the rest of your life?

_____

_____

_____

_____

How will you use your multidimensional magic to create a meaningful life and to change the world?

_____

_____

_____

_____

In what ways are you playing small?

_____

_____

_____

_____

You have magnificence within you; what does it look like?

_____

_____

_____

_____

What is your destiny?

_____

_____

_____

_____

What kind of legacy will you leave behind?

_____

_____

_____

_____

What are your deepest fears?

_____

_____

_____

_____

If you unleash your true power, what will happen?

_____

_____

_____

_____

What have the messengers in your life told you about your destiny?

_____

_____

_____

_____

What do you need to believe so you can picture and achieve that destiny?

_____

_____

_____

_____

What will your life be like when you finally unleash your significance?

_____

_____

_____

_____

ABOUT THE AUTHOR
CATRICE M. JACKSON, MS, LMHP, LPC

INTERNATIONAL ANTI-RACISM EDUCATOR | SPEAKER | AUTHOR | FREEDOM FIGHTER
AMERICA'S #1 EXPERT ON WHITE WOMAN VIOLENCE

Chief Conductor at ***Harriet's Dream*** ® *&*
Host of Black Couch Conversations

"If you don't have an anti-racism plan, you plan to be racist."
—Catrice M. Jackson #Catriceology

Catrice is a Black woman who loves, centers, and celebrates blackness every day while unapologetically living her best Black life. She is the CEO of Catriceology® Enterprises, LLC; the Chief Conductor at Harriet's Dream®, a racial trauma healing and wellness center for Black women; and the host of Black Couch Conversations, a Black-ass podcast for Black folks with a psychological twist. Catrice is also the creator of SHETalks WETalk Race Talks for Women and the author of ten books, including *Antagonists, Advocates and Allies; White Spaces Missing Faces; The Becky Code*; and *Unf*ckablewith*. As an anti-racism speaker and educator, Catrice serves up strong medicine and hard truths in a straight-up, on-the-rocks, no-chaser style to eliminate the lethal infection of racism. Unbothered by naysayers and unflinching in her approach, Catrice's dedication to Black people is the motivation behind her personal movement, Justice Is Love.

EDUCATION
- PhD, Organizational Psychology, Walden University (dissertation in progress).
- MS, Human Services/Counseling, Bellevue University.
- Licensed Mental Health Practitioner (LMHP).
- Licensed Professional Counselor (LPC).
- BS, Criminal Justice Administration, Bellevue University.
- Licensed Practical Nurse, Western Iowa Technical Community College.
- Certified Domestic Abuse and Sexual Assault Advocate, Trainer, and Speaker.

SOCIAL MEDIA CONTACTS

FACEBOOK
@CatriceJacksonSpeaks
@therealcatriceology
@blackwomanbadassery

TWITTER
@Beckyologist

INSTAGRAM
@Catriceology

YOUTUBE
@Catriceology1

WEBSITES
www.catriceology.com
www.shetalkswetalk.com
www.catriceologyenterprises.com
www.thebeckycode.com

RADIO
SHETALKS WETALK RADIO
www.blogtalkradio.com/shetalkswetalk

PODCAST
BLACK COUCH CONVERSATIONS ON SOUNDCLOUD
https://soundcloud.com/catriceology

OTHER CATRICEOLOGY® BOOKS
All Books Sold on Amazon

Unf*ckablewith
The Becky Code
White Spaces Missing Faces
Antagonists, Advocates and Allies
Unleash Your Significance

The Billboard Brand
Brand Like A BOSSLady
The Art of Fear-Free Living
Delicious!
Soul Eruption!

HIRE CATRICE FOR SPEAKING AND EDUCATION
Catrice is available for speaking opportunities, radio and podcast segments, organizational training, anti-racism education, and leadership consulting.

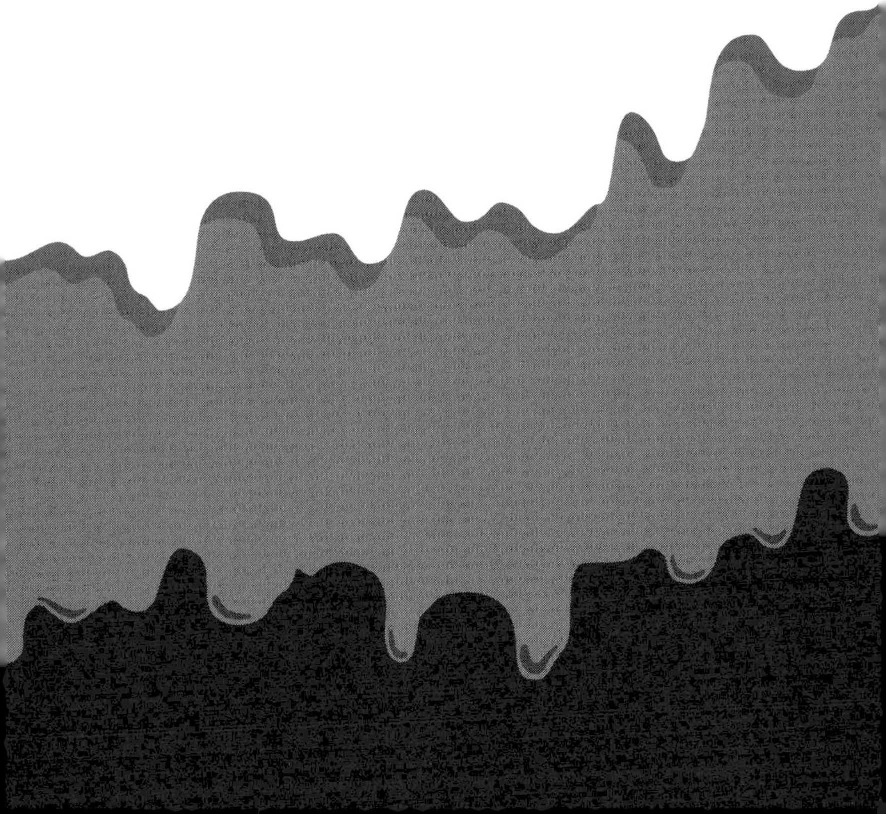

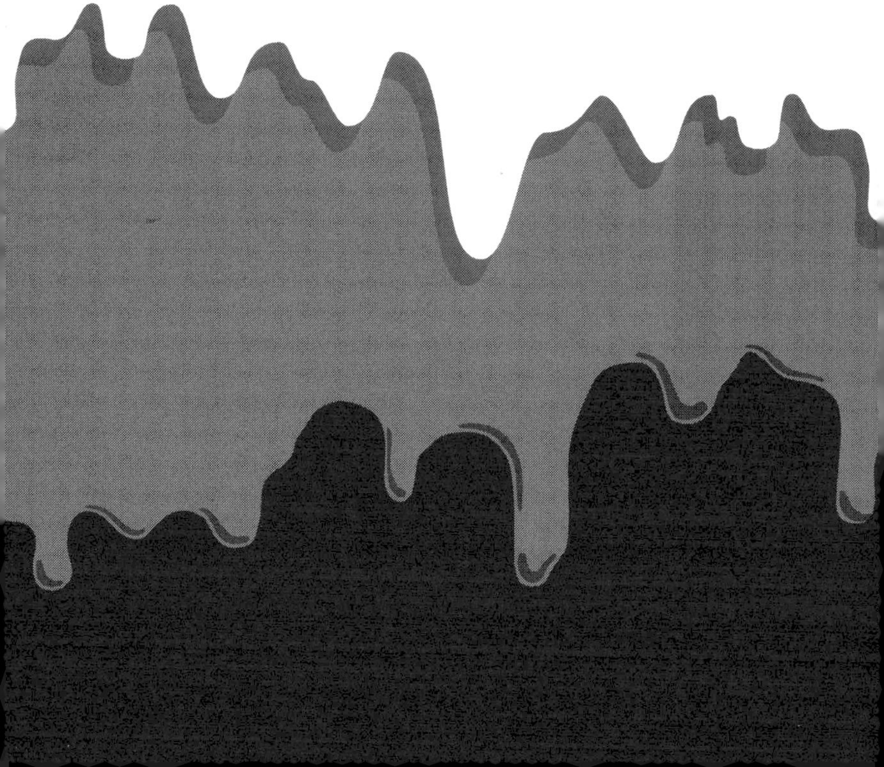

Printed in Great Britain
by Amazon